*From the Foreword:*

Dr Marjory Foyle ... has been one of the most influential psychiatrists in the world. She has nurtured new treatment services in developing countries, teaching and training on mental health issues all over the world, and looking after and investigating the psychological problems of missionaries and other expatriates ...

This is the account of someone who throughout life has put her trust in God – absolutely, unflinchingly and whole-heartedly – and, despite numerous adventures, God has never failed her. It is whimsical, humorous but above all inspiring. I expect this story will change lives. Once engrossed, I could not put it down.

**Andrew C P Sims**
*Emeritus Professor of Psychiatry, Leeds*
*and former President of The Royal College of Psychiatrists*

This is a fascinating story written by a remarkable woman of God. Marjory Foyle covers experiences as diverse as delivering a goat, meeting Mother Teresa, overcoming depression and achieving a major academic thesis at the age of 78. Anyone who appreciates how God can help us in our weakness will enjoy this lively book. It is full of spiritual and psychological 'nuggets'. Marjory Foyle's humour and compassion are present on every page.

**M Dominic Beer**
*Consultant Psychiatrist in Challenging Behaviour*
*and Intensive Care Psychiatry, Oxleas NHS Trust*

Marjory's story reflects her character: compassionate but very honest, dignified but gently subversive ... and all shot through with a humble, but sometimes 'wicked' sense of humour! God's grace is clearly seen through the life of an ordinary woman who simply takes God at his word. The result is a life which impacts countless individuals around the globe – and, more amazingly, which enjoys an increasingly close and honest friendship with God. Marjory is a constant challenge, inspiration and encouragement to me – I'm sure you'll find the same as you share her story of life with the Living God.

**Jenny Brown**
*Senior Associate Minister (Training & World Mission),*
*All Souls Church, Langham Place, London*

*i*

I was an Interserve Partner in Nepal in the 1970s when I first met Marjory Foyle as I, with my family, passed through Lucknow on our way into India for a holiday. She made an immediate impact. She was never pretentious despite her reputation, gifts and abilities; she was always generous and interested in us; and she was most certainly always interesting as a person.

Despite her gentle and unassuming exterior Marjory has become recognised world-wide for her expertise and has been a major player in the world-wide revolution in the standards of support care for those living and working in other cultures. She has been of great help both to individuals who have sought her counsel and to organisations who have needed her help – and her challenge to change practices and recognise the special needs of both adults and children as they live in different cultures and as they move from one culture to another.

Marjory describes herself as a 'troubled child whom God met'. In this book, with typically self-deprecating humour and with insight into herself and others, she traces the ways in which God met her and shaped her so that this troubled child became somebody who achieved extraordinary things for God. Her love for Jesus and her simple faith in him shines through. Marjory describes life as a series of circles and she shows how she learnt from each one and allowed God to shape her for the future. I'm sure that everybody who reads this book will find something in it for themselves, for although Marjory is a very special person, she is also a very normal person, and we can all be encouraged and challenged that the same God who used Marjory can also use us. Could it be you?

**Richard Clark**
*National Director, Interserve England and Wales*

Marjory Foyle is a doctor of many parts, and a woman of many lives. Her greatest achievement is interpreting, understanding and ministering to the needs of expatriate Christians, both adults and families. Her insights as a hands-on psychiatrist, whether through books, seminars or face-to-face contact have helped thousands of missionaries and contributed significantly to the global understanding of expatriate stress.

**Ted Lankester**
*Director of Healthcare, InterHealth, London*

Not many of us are awarded our PhD at 78! Marjory seems to have packed into her incredible life since retirement more than the average person manages over a whole life-time ... and well into her 80s she's still asking the question what does God want of me next? Perhaps that's her secret – and a question we too must never stop asking.

**Martin Lee**
*Director, Global Connections, London*

# Can it be me?

To Paul & Rebecca
with love from

Marjory F. Foyle

This book is dedicated to my family on earth and in heaven,
and to my many friends around the world

# Can it be me?

by Marjory F Foyle

CAN IT BE ME?
© 2006 by Marjory Foyle
Reprinted 2007

Published by Christian Medical Fellowship,
6-8 Marshalsea Road, London, England SE1
www.cmf.org.uk

Cover design by S2 Design and Advertising
Cover photo © Alison Whitlock 2006

ISBNs:
0 906747 36 8
978 0 906747 36 0

All Scripture quotations, unless otherwise indicated,
are taken from the Holy Bible, New International
Version NIV. Copyright 1973, 1978, 1984 by
International Bible Society. Used by permission.

Body typeset in Palatino 9.5/12

Typeset by Dr R C J Carling

Printed in Great Britain by Stanley L Hunt (printers) Ltd,
Midland Road, Rushden, Northants

# Contents

# Foreword

'*Can it be Me?*... expresses my surprise at finding myself doing all sorts of things I would never have thought possible...'

Dr Marjory Foyle, towards the end of a long life and through many diverse careers, has been one of the most influential psychiatrists in the world. She has nurtured new treatment services in developing countries, teaching and training on mental health issues all over the world, and looking after and investigating the psychological problems of missionaries and other expatriates. Her unobtrusive counsel has resulted in improvements in practice in many countries. She is an amazing lady; she submitted her thesis and obtained the degree of MD (medical PhD) in her late 70s.

Biography, especially Christian biography, can sometimes be unreal and dispiriting reading. This autobiography is neither; it is absolutely honest, extremely funny and is an account spanning more than 60 years of Marjory 'living in partnership with God'. She describes her own depressive illness when grossly overworked as a missionary doctor in India; this led to her training in psychiatry and her subsequent work. She asked God to take away her stammer, but he helped her to address big meetings despite it and it even became a blessing:

'... people had accepted me, stammer and all, and years after I had left I heard that some of the women had come to the Hospital to ask "Where is the doctor that speaks like a baby? She really understands us".'

Her story comes across as a very modern one: she was the product of a broken family and brought up by a single mother; as a young woman she was crippled by shyness and low self-esteem; she suffered from depressive illness; she felt that she was not much good at being an evangelist; she had difficulty reintegrating into British culture after a decade in India. She came to God through 'this huge need to belong, to be loved in a new way'. She did her daily work feeling that God was close beside her and helping her.

Shortly after her 80th birthday she read Jeremiah 30:21: 'Who is he who will devote himself to be close to me?'

'I stood up in my bedroom study and said out loud, "I will and I do", and then I laughed because anyone watching me might think I was decidedly weird, although God understood what it was all about!'

Her latest ministry is talking to people on the street and on the underground, often about God, 'because I am so obviously old and harmless I have never had any trouble'. However, she is sensitive 'because there is nothing worse than turning into an interfering busybody!'

I strongly recommend you to read on. This is the account of someone who throughout life has put her trust in God – absolutely, unflinchingly and whole-heartedly – and, despite numerous adventures, God has never failed her. It is whimsical, humorous but above all inspiring. I expect this story will change lives. Once engrossed, I could not put it down.

**Andrew CP Sims**
*Emeritus Professor of Psychiatry, Leeds*
*and former President of The Royal College of Psychiatrists*
*September 2006*

# Introduction

My sister and I often talked about people who wrote autobiographies. We agreed that they must be proud and self centred. I am therefore surprised and a little guilty to find myself doing just what we condemned!

Over the years many people have said to me, 'You should write your life story so people can learn more about how God works in human lives'. Finally I decided to ask God to give me a sign by prompting a series of people to ask me within one calendar week to write my autobiography, and he did exactly that. Four separate people on four successive days suddenly asked me a propos of nothing to write my autobiography, and my family on earth gave permission, so here it is.

**Marjory Foyle**

# My beginnings

My earliest memory is of waddling down a street in Tredegar, Wales, wearing a bright orange knitted suit and a cap with a grey pom-pom on top. We were going to see the coal mine, and I dimly remember the deep dark hole with a lift going up and down full of dirty men. My father was the Methodist minister in the town, which at that time contained two very distinguished people. One was the young Aneurin Bevan who learnt his speaking skills at the Methodist Men's weekly meeting. He later became a famous Labour politician. The other was one of the local doctors, A J Cronin, who wrote several famous novels such as *The Citadel*. I do not remember either of them, but boasted about my Tredegar connections with them during relevant lessons at school.

The orange suit with the grey pompom

My father came from the same family as Foyle's bookshop in London. He and the founders, William and Gilbert, were first cousins, but there was some sort of quarrel between them so we never really got to know the famous Foyles. Jane Austen of *Pride and Prejudice* fame appears somewhere distantly in the family tree, and my father was very proud of these connections. His personal family background was not very happy, due, I believe, to chronic illness, but we rarely met his relatives. He himself was a gifted man, a good writer and preacher, and from him I got my enduring love of history.

After becoming a Methodist minister my father went abroad as a missionary, first to India and then to the Caribbean. During

one of his home leaves he met my mother. She was of Scottish and Cornish descent and had a secure early childhood. Her father was the Cornish half, a wonderful man who became a ship's captain. My mother told me that everyone who knew him loved him, and many passengers sailed with him regularly on the USA/ UK route. We have a scroll of gratitude from the passengers of the liner he took safely over to USA in a very bad storm, plus a silver headed walking stick.

How he met my grand-mother was a romantic story. During a few days shore-leave in Glasgow he saw my grand-mother in a tea shop. When she went out he asked one of the shop girls how he could

My Cornish grandfather, Captain James Peters

meet her. Being directed to go to the Presbyterian Church evening youth meeting he duly turned up, met her, and later married her. They adored each other, although my grandmother could not cope with the tiny Cornish village of Portscatho from which he came. So they decided she should return to Scotland with her first child, my mother, so that she could have the support of her old friends while he was at sea.

Granny was a lovely person, upright and honest. She was deeply spiritual, and, when I was sitting with her during her last illness, I heard her repeat many long portions of Scripture. She was partly Highland where some people have what they call 'the second sight', a sort of special insight, and she told me a curious story about her husband's death. He was recalled to the Merchant

Navy as a ship's captain in 1914 when the First World War began, and survived until May 1918 when his ship was torpedoed. Everyone got into lifeboats, and using the new contraption, radio, notified Scotland they were all safe. My grandmother was told the good news, but in the middle of the night she woke up and saw her husband standing at the foot of the bed. He said to her 'Don't worry Jeannie, you will be all right and will bring the children up very well'. Next day she heard he was dead, having drowned trying to rescue important Government papers from his cabin before the ship went down.

My grandparents had three children, all girls, my mother being the oldest. She was very intelligent, and became the first woman in Scotland to gain a Masters degree in education via the 'pupil teacher' route. This enabled people with not much money to gain a University education by working part-time in a school and attending University the rest of the week. She was also very brave. Just before her father drowned she herself set sail to the Caribbean to marry my father, a very unusual thing for a young girl of her generation to do. My brother Arthur, also known as Monty, and my sister Edith Victoria, known as Vicky, were both born in the Caribbean. Because my parents lived on a Dutch island and wanted the children to be born British, my mother sailed over to Nevis in a small ship during the eighth month, taking over three hours to get there. The first time it was March, probably lovely weather but three years later it was June, just before the hurricane season, so it was not much fun for her.

My beautiful grandmother,
Jeannie Peters

In 1920 the family returned to the UK and my father was appointed to a church in Dorset. I was born in 1921. Many things that have happened to me have had a funny side to them and my birth was no exception. The midwife had just been to see my mother and was on her way home when my mother had one huge pain. She thought it was the fish she ate for lunch but instead I appeared, causing the midwife to return at the run to get me breathing. From then on we moved regularly, as was the pattern in Wesleyan Methodism in those days. In the next twelve years we moved from Dorset to Wales, to two places in Yorkshire, to Northamptonshire, and then back to Wales. It was there that my parents' stormy marriage finally broke up. My mother took us to live in a horrible small apartment in a rough area of London. During this period there was a traumatic legal procedure to ensure my mother had custody of the children, so Granny came and lived with us for a time to give help and support. How I hated that apartment. I longed for the country, because before the split-up we had lived in one of the most beautiful parts of Wales. One day walking unhappily down a London street I saw a bus marked, as I thought, 'London Bog'. 'Cheers,' I thought , 'if there is a bog there must be some country near by', but then I came to know it was London Bdg (Bridge), one of the busiest railway stations in the heart of London.

The church decided to continue to pay for our education in Methodist Boarding schools, my brother going to Kingswood in Bath, and my sister and I to Trinity Hall in Southport. This was truly a godsend, for although my mother went back to teaching to support us, she could never have paid for such a good education. My brother was brilliant, winning scholarships and prizes everywhere, but my sister and I were conscientious plodders, very rarely winning anything that helped us financially. That we all finally graduated and made useful contributions was a tribute to my mother's tenacity and determination that we should be well educated.

My childhood had a profound influence on me, although it was to be forty years before I began to understand it and to come to terms with what had happened. The first problem was that my brother and I both inherited a genetic stammer, which my sister escaped. He was very good at everything so it made little difference to him, but I suffered. I was small, had straight hair which was definitely 'out' in those days, and due to the difficult atmosphere at home both before and after the separation was never able to ask children home to play. My consolations were my dolls, and the ability to write. I wrote poems and stories as soon as I could read and write, and I think these brought me some sense of personal value, but overall, as a rather plain stammering child with few social gifts, I felt very lonely.

To make things worse, because I was the last child living at home, I had to bear the brunt of the quarrels and shouting that went on. My sister and I had already experienced these, and we both dimly recognised the potential for violence between our parents. From the beginning my sister was my comfort and help. She made it her role to 'look after little Marj', and continued to do this until she died aged 85. But after she went to boarding school I had to cope alone. I remember how startled my grandmother was when I told her that if I went away to boarding school I was sure my father would try to kill my mother. She did not believe me, but that is exactly what happened. A few months later, when I was away at school, I had a week of nightmares of my father trying to kill my mother. I later discovered that this was the exact period during which my father reached the end of his tether and tried to murder her, until she managed to escape and run to a neighbour's house.

My mother's graduation

It took me many years to work out what had gone wrong and I want to be fair to both parents. I knew my mother regretted the marriage, but never knew enough about my father to work out his problems. I believe he was a genuine Christian, was very intelligent and wrote well. My brother once told me that when he preached he was so good that he 'held the audience in his hand'. By what I learned later, I recognised that he had been pretty knocked about by unpleasant experiences at University, and by his difficult family background. As marital partners I think they were genuinely incompatible, becoming rivals rather than supporters until they both finally reached breaking point. When I grew up I only saw him once. He suddenly appeared at a meeting where I was about to speak. I recognised him instantly and asked one of the platform party to go down and warn my mother. After the meeting she spoke to him and sent him away. My greatest consolation now is that they have come to understand and forgive each other in heaven but it was not until many years later that I dealt with my own emotional reactions to the whole thing.

I do not want to give the impression that we children were neglected. We were cared for, fed and clothed, taken out on treats, helped with our homework, and all the usual things of a normal family. The abnormal thing was that it was mostly done by my mother. The only times I remember speaking to my father were when he took us walking on the moors, and when I spent a week alone with him during which we went on cycle rides together. Neither of my parents were contact people in terms of hugging or kissing us, and looking back I think we did suffer emotional deprivation in this sense. However, that was not very unusual in families in the 1920s, but it made an impact on me because I was so frightened of the whole situation. But I do remember the security of having German measles (rubella), being tucked up in bed, and my mother reading 'The Rainbow Comic' to me, protesting vigorously that I read such junk!

In a later chapter I shall be explaining how I got all this sorted out, but at this point it is understandable that I was a lonely child with little opportunity or capacity to make friends. Boarding schools could sometimes be cruel places, despite excellent staff, and at mine you were either very popular, mildly popular, or not at all popular! I was in the last category, as I once discovered. But I never gave up on life. I decided I would go my own way, concentrate on what I enjoyed, and make friends with others in the bottom group. My stammer persisted, I could not read aloud in class, but I could sing and boast about my aunt who was premier mezzo-soprano in the Glasgow Operatic Society. When I was 13, my brother decided to take my musical education in hand. I was learning the violin (excruciatingly I am afraid), so he taught me to listen to music carefully and to read complicated musical scores. He took me to the promenade concerts in the old Queens Hall, London, where I fell in love with Paul Beard, the first violinist. Because I was so small I stood on a huge encyclopaedia, and would gaze adoringly at him hoping that one day he would look at me – alas he never did! I grew to enjoy opera and classical music, Bach in particular sending me into ecstasies. He still does, and when we have Bach voluntaries at church I just sit there glowing. From an early age I wrote poetry which was sometimes published in the school magazine, I won a first prize in English Literature, and shot the two winning goals in an important school hockey match, but these were my only claims to fame.

All this helped me to emerge as a person, but it did not really make me feel any happier. Both before and after the split-up there were multiple problems at home. My sister and I were in different sections of the school a few miles apart, and I did not really feel free to talk to anyone else. There were no official school counsellors in those days, but the school nurse was very kind to me, particularly in the nightmare period when I must have looked pretty grim. So I plodded on, struggling with my difficulty in making relationships, and returning to a very lonely life in the London flat in the holidays. I knew absolutely no one of my own age in London, and rarely saw my older Cornish relatives whose father owned the local ironmonger's shop. There was another Cornish senior Aunt, Rose, whose husband had the distinction of managing the laundry to which all the Royal household sent their dirty clothes. This section was walled off from the ordinary laundry, but I used to feel a sense of awe as I passed it and thought back to Queen Victoria's voluminous garments being washed there. Auntie Rose was a lovely lady who used to give me treats in London. We went to a shop called Derry and Toms, very swanky, with a tea-room where the ceiling kept changing colour in beautiful patterns.

My mother and I were never really able to talk. This was not a part of her background, but we did have a very happy social relationship and I knew she cared about my welfare. Where she got the money from I do not know, but she sometimes took me away for a week's holiday by the sea, often staying in a really nice hotel where we 'dressed for dinner'. One year she bought me the dress of my dreams from a real grown-up shop, and we even spent a weekend at an expensive hotel in Oxford. How she afforded it was a mystery, but possibly it was a teacher's 'special offer' if they had them in those days. Because hugging and kissing were not a part of our family culture, I never felt emotionally loved by anyone except my wonderful elocution teacher who tried to help me with my speech. We really talked, and I was thrilled when she used one of my poems to train her oral speech chorus. Unfortunately my mother could not afford her fees so after about two years I regretfully had to stop seeing her.

One good thing came out of this childhood pattern. I learned to amuse myself during the holidays when my mother was working and I was home alone, Monty and Vicky, my brother and sister, being occupied elsewhere with their studies. We had good radios by that time, better than the old 'cat's whisker' headphone set we began with! I listened avidly. Anything and everything was grist to my mill. I heard Len Hutton get the highest score in cricket, concerts from the BBC, plays, Children's Hour, news, anything and everything, although I turned it off if it was scary. I also learned how to go out alone, and cope with the ordinary problems of living in London. Although at that time I was self-sufficient, not God-sufficient, the skills I learned in that London flat during my adolescence were definitely God-given. They became very useful to me when I was unavoidably alone during part of my work in India and when I later began extensive travelling. Things became easier for all of us when we moved to a much better house with a park behind it and a nice little garden. I do not wish to give the impression I was neglected, we went away on holidays, and I was well cared for, but there

My brother, sister and me, in descending order

was no venue through which I could meet local people of my own age. My mother was far too busy and tired to entertain very much, other than occasionally seeing her Cornish relations.

After my parents split up, we tried to go to the local Methodist church, but it was always problematical since we could not explain where we came from, and where my father was. To be separated from one's husband was unusual in those days, and if it was discovered he was a Methodist minister things could have become very difficult indeed. So we gradually stopped going. During my school years I had a few religious interests, following the usual pattern of school prayers and Sunday services, and feeling sentimental in the dim light of evening church. I decided to join the Church, which was a Methodist rite of passage, but there was little teaching and I gradually drifted away from religion. And anyway, despite joining the church, I had more or less decided by the age of twelve that there might be a God but if so he didn't care anything about me. I gradually entered a phase of agnosticism during which I wrote such bitter poetry that someone who read it was very alarmed and contacted my sister.

The school years went by, and I began to think of my future career. My sister was studying to be a doctor and I finally decided I wanted to do the same. By this time my brother was nearly qualified as an architect, and due to scholarships and awards was totally self-supporting, apart from having to return home during a rather lean financial period.

I was once instrumental in saving my brother's life. I was at university, and while sitting in a lecture had a strong compulsion to go home, where he was living at the time. This was so strong that I acted on it immediately. When I got home I found my brother confused and unable to recognise me, with a high temperature and a body covered with huge red spots. I immediately phoned the doctor who diagnosed meningococcal meningitis. Until a few months before my brother got it this was a fatal illness, but sulphonamides by injection had just arrived on the medical scene. He was one of the first to have these injectable life-savers, and after a long convalescence returned to work as good as new. I felt I might have inherited a bit of my Grandmother's 'second sight', hence the compulsion to go home, and was so glad to be able to help.

Once my mother realised I wanted to be a doctor she again began to look around for financial help. She got bits and pieces of scholarship money for both my sister and me and, since tuition was free and I would live at home, we felt we could just manage. I was interviewed by the Dean of The London School of Medicine for Women (Royal Free Hospital) where my sister was now a second year student, and was offered a place. Everything was going well, but unfortunately the Second World War began just before I was due to begin my studies. The medical school with all its staff was evacuated from London to Scotland and, when we were informed of this, we realised that there was no way my mother could pay for two of us to study and live away from home. Student jobs were unheard of in those days so I went sadly back to school to try to work out the best thing to do. One golden day a few weeks later my mother sent me a telegram saying 'Join medical school, sending money, love Mummy'. My only clothes were a very old hat and one skirt and blouse but off I went with a small suitcase and my violin. I arrived at St Andrews, where the famous golf course is, with nowhere to stay and no chance of registering at University till the next day. But as I explained earlier, I was used to coping alone, so I wandered into a rather sleazy public house and, despite this being strictly against my teetotal upbringing, asked for a room. They took pity on me and gave me a room at very low cost because it was over the bar, where the customers sang drunkenly for many hours before being chucked out at closing time. Next day I joined the medical school and began a new life.

# 2

# A double learning curve

My first year at University seemed like a marvellous dream from which I expected to awake any minute. St Andrews was magnificent: old buildings, history under every footstep, glorious sea and coast line. Anyone who has seen the opening sequence of the movie 'Chariots of Fire' will remember the sands the athletic team ran along, with St Andrews in the background. My attic bedroom window looked along the whole length of these sands. The neighbouring dunes were filled with skylarks, and it was not long before I was taking a daily walk along them, thrilled to bits with everything. I shared the attic bedroom with a girl I knew from school. Comfort was not the word one would use about it, and one morning after a night-long blizzard we woke up to two inches of snow on the bedroom floor. But I loved everything – the studies, the independence, the opportunity to take up a sport (fencing), and the whole academic atmosphere created by an old established university in a smallish historic town. I attended the university chapel more for the architecture than anything else, and began to make a few friends. One of these lived in the same house, an interesting person called Mary Stokes, and we have now been friends for 55 years. Fairly early in our friendship she said she was a committed Christian, but I never paid any attention to anything she said about it. She had an exotic background in Greece and Turkey, and was a magnificent swimmer. Her birthday was in February, and she asked me to come and stand on the shore while she went into the open air swimming pool on the edge of the crashing sea. It was perishing cold on the sands let alone in the water, but after about 20 minutes she came back as red as a lobster but very pleased with her swim. Later Mary became a medical missionary in Iran and then began a career as a well-known and respected obstetrician and gynaecologist in London, maintaining her strong Christian commitment throughout.

One of my good friends in St Andrews was the keeper of the Castle. I used to go there to study. I think he realised I had very little money, so he would ask me to go and buy him a 'slider' (an ice cream wafer) and to get one for myself. These were blissful moments in the sun, by the sea, eating ice cream with a friend, and then returning to my books. I also made another friend, Gertrude Klatzkin, who comes up again later in my story. My laboratory companion was Liza Frankl, a distinguished psychologist and refugee from Hitler's Germany. Her brother was the famous Victor Frankl who was incarcerated in Belsen and Auschwitz, and survived to create a new school of psychotherapy. Altogether I found that such people were very interesting, and it all expanded my somewhat limited horizons in a very helpful way.

I think my feeling of learning to live a normal life was more than just growing up. It was so relaxing to be able to get on with my job without carrying constant anxiety about my parents. I naturally worried about my mother in war-time London, but she wrote cheerful letters and was glad I was well settled. I spent Christmas with my sister in Aberdeen, a few hours north of St Andrews and *much* colder. My sister lived in the YWCA hostel, and we were amused to find a collection of empty beer bottles on our doorstep the morning after Hogmanay, the New Year festival. Jokers had picked up all the bottles they could find to put on our doorstep, to tease the 'Young Women Christians' who in that generation were not supposed to drink alcohol. My sister and I, as usual, were short of money and had not enough to sign our New Year wishes telegram home with both our names. So we combined them and signed Marjedith, at which the clerk looked at us suspiciously, but we sweetly wished him a 'Happy New Year' and he smiled and sent it.

Then it was back to the grindstone, Biology, Chemistry and Physics. Here I met my second major deficit. I cannot understand anything mathematical apart from mental arithmetic which we practised to exhaustion at school. I can count to 20 with my shoes off and use a calculator if it's more than 20, and that's about it. So I solved the problem of physics by learning all the theorems by heart, making me word perfect, and not doing any of the riders attached, ie the sums that examined how you used the theorem. This gave me exactly 50% marks, enough to pass the exam. So hurdle number one to being a doctor was over.

I went back home for the long summer vacation, saying a regretful goodbye to St Andrews. The medical school had decided to move again and reunite the first and second years in Exeter, south west England. I now had to get a job for three months and offered my services as an untrained nurse in a local ward for the elderly bedridden. They were so short of staff they took me on. I got paid fairly well, was given one meal a day, a uniform and a little very basic training. I owe them a big debt for teaching me to test urines and then letting me get on with it, and especially for teaching me how to give a bed bath and to care for the backs of predominantly incontinent old women lying in bed all day. In my later career the nurses were often surprised at how much I knew about bed baths and general nursing care. While I was working there the real war began, and we experienced bombing for the first time. Nurses going home after duty were not considered 'essential to the war effort' so we were not given tin hats. My mother and brother used to come to meet me holding saucepans and frying pans over their heads and bringing one for me. Although I was a total oddity in the ward I enjoyed myself, and started learning how to approach and help many different kinds of people.

During this period I had another brief incursion into religion, but only because I really liked the look of the Canadian pastor of a local church. So I used to sit and adore him while he was trying to teach us to adore and love God. When I moved on, to Exeter this time, I soon forgot the lovely Canadian and thought little about the God he was presenting.

Exeter is a Cathedral city in beautiful Devonshire. As we did in St Andrews, we took all our own staff with us and worked in premises borrowed from the University. On arrival we were housed in the large hostel for women students. I stayed there for two weeks, but then my mother wrote and explained she had never agreed to this, and could not afford it. So I and an impoverished friend, with whom I had been at school, went to see our own medical school officials. They explained to Exeter staff that we were an independent unit and therefore not subject to the rule that first year students had to live in the hostel. My friend knew the local Methodist minister and we discovered they were being compelled by the Government to house two people in their spare room as part of the war effort. Rather than having munitions workers who smelled of gunpowder and worked night shifts they were delighted to take us as their official lodgers.

Living in their house proved to be the beginning of a new life for me in every way. They were a lovely couple. He was English and she was Scottish. They quarrelled like all people do, but always made it up, and their love for each other and their two children was a deep and constant thing. I watched them very carefully although they never realised it. I was trying to learn how couples could relate together, how my own parenting could have been had the troubles not arisen. I decided to attend the church and see what he was talking about. It was fascinating, not brilliant rhetorical preaching but good solid stuff that we needed to know if we were to live properly. We began to argue (poor man, he got it every meal time I was at home), but they were loving and patient with their lodgers. Their children also tolerated us, one of them allowing herself to be prodded and poked as we learnt surface anatomy. I decided it might be worthwhile having a new look at Christianity, so went along to the Student Christian Movement (SCM) meetings at irregular intervals. I wanted to see if there was any connection between the Christianity I saw practised in the home, and the Christian faith. I found the SCM people fairly sensible, most of their concerns being social issues rather than the meaning and content of the Christian faith.

My arguments with the Methodist minister continued, becoming stronger each week, and I went on attending his church to see if I could understand what created the loving atmosphere in their home and relationship. The climax came one night in the Methodist Church where my host preached an admirable sermon, although I have no memory of its content. At the end he invited anyone who wanted to belong to Jesus to go forward. I felt a strong compulsion to do so, and rushed out of my seat and down the aisle to the communion rail where I stood crying my eyes out. I had no idea what was going on, just that I was overwhelmed by a personal need to belong. Mary Stokes joined me to make an act of rededication, and Gertrude Klatzkin whom I mentioned earlier, a Jewess, also came forward. The Minster spoke to each one of us, said the final benediction, gave us a booklet and that was that.

Next day I was surprised to receive an invitation to tea from a Miss Norah Nixon. She was the women's travelling secretary of the student Christian organisation, then called IVF (Inter-Varsity Fellowship) but now known in the UK as UCCF (Universities and Colleges' Christian Fellowship). I learned later that she had arrived on a regular visit, someone had told her about me, and she felt it would be good if we met. We sat in the window of a tea-shop overlooking the cathedral, and she explained the gospel to me. She told me Jesus loved me, that he had died for my sin, for my loneliness and need, and that by believing in him I was given a new life which he would share with me through the Holy Spirit taking up residence in my heart. He was promising me a life in which I could serve him, find refuge, and begin to grow in God. We talked and talked, periodically ordering more tea to keep the waitress a bit happier. The whole time she was telling me what the Bible said as if it was a really true book. At the end she gave me a book to read, and a piece of advice I have operated on all my life: 'Try to read the Bible and talk to God naturally in prayer every day, and never sit down to read without a pen in your hand. This shows God you want to learn.' She then linked me up with a local student in the IVF, and she herself remained my good friend for as long as she lived. Her trademark was a famous hat, she never bought a new one as far as I know, and I feel sure it must be on a pedestal somewhere in heaven!

The café in Exeter where Norah Nixon and I sat for three hours

After saying goodbye to Norah I went for a walk. I realised I had not come to Jesus because of a major sense of sin, but out of enormous personal need. I needed someone to help me live, to change my personality and help me forge good relationships, to look after my inner loneliness by being always with me. I thought of a verse Norah had quoted 'I will never leave you nor forsake you'. I could never be alone again. I might feel lonely but was never actually going to be alone. There was a security ahead, a sense of cohesion and purpose, and I would become a member not only of my own family but of a far larger worldwide one, the family of those who accepted Jesus as their Lord and Saviour. I did not of course put all this into words, but as I look back on it today these are the small seeds that God put into my mind and heart as I walked, went home, ate supper, studied and went to bed. Next morning I got up a little earlier than usual, picked up my school Bible and went to university via the cathedral. I found a warm place and opened the Bible at random. It was Psalm 72 in the old King James Version. I knew little of the context in which it was written but certain words shot out at me. 'He shall come down like rain on the mown grass', and I had often felt somewhat mown down during my past life. 'He shall deliver the needy when he cries, the poor also and him that has no helper.' I was exaggerating of course. I had known helpers, I had been supported, and I was not all that poor. But nothing had filled the gaping inner void I always seemed to have, and these words were like oil pouring down inside.

I got in contact with the local student whose name Norah had given me, and in a few days' time decided to join the IVF group. From them I began learning something about what it really means, according to the Bible, to be a Christian. I began to realise that when Jesus died on the cross it was not just a brave deed, the rationale for which I could not understand. He died as the Son of God, to restore the world to relationship with God, which our sin had spoiled. I learned that Jesus died for me personally, to restore me to fellowship with a living, loving, God, and that I could find out all about this by reading the Bible, his word to me, and by praying to him and learning to trust him. My local contact also put me in touch with Drs Charles and Norah Sims, a husband and wife doctor team who cared for Christian medical student welfare by a regular Sunday evening meeting. It was a great day for me many years later when their baby son became the President of the Royal College of Psychiatrists, and it felt as if not only was he being honoured for his own fantastic qualities, but also as a tribute to the care his parents had given to so many people.

Being me I went at religion 'hammer and tongs' as we say in England, and got a bit worn out after a bad bout of flu. So Dr Norah Sims was called in by my hostess, and after examining me she read me the riot act about living a balanced life, which must also include time for fresh air and exercise, and for periodically doing nothing! I never forgot that advice. I continued to go to the cathedral every morning for private reading and prayer, and when the verger saw me coming he stoked up the ancient boiler to keep me a bit warmer. I began getting proper exercise, and also began fire watching in the cathedral, a rather spooky but interesting experience. Major bombing raids usually began with fire bombs so groups of watchers would try to put them out quickly before the big bombers arrived. This meant wandering over the roof of the cathedral, and to get there I had to go through a really eerie part of the clergy office downstairs where all the white gowns worn by the choir gleamed in a frightening way. So I usually ran through and shot upstairs to relieve the person on duty. Nothing much happened during my time there, although the whole city was badly bombed just after I had moved on.

During this period I was making friends, driving my room companion to distraction by my new interest in 'religion', and working hard at my studies. I then discovered that despite the war, student Christian conferences were still being held in Oxford, and I decided to save up some money and go. A marvellous man with a small guest house managed to feed us all outside his house, and God kept the rain away. The meetings opened a new door for me. I had never heard such clear explanations of the meaning of being a Christian, such erudite yet simple and reasonable ways of explaining the Bible, and I learned that it was possible to live an ordinary human life with God as guide and companion. I decided after much thought that even though there were huge chunks of the Bible I did not understand, I would accept the whole as the word of God to me as an individual, and try to understand it more as time went by.

Students talked a lot about 'witnessing to others' but I was not much good at it. I felt hampered by my speech and my lack of social skills. But one day I was invited to go with other students to help conduct a ward service in a local hospital. The leader was a formidable middle-aged medical student, a friend of my sister's – her story would demand another book! She knew nothing about me except that I had recently become a Christian, and as we moved to another ward she suddenly turned to me and said 'You are the next speaker'. What on earth was I to do? I had never done anything like that before, but I felt I should have a go. I asked someone where the parable of the prodigal son was in the Bible, asked them to read it for us, and then stood up and spoke! I am sure I stammered, but I spoke out loud, completed my little talk, and felt it was right for me to be doing this. I was absolutely weak at the knees as I finished, so I said goodbye to the others and went straight back to my room. I knelt down by my bed and asked God to show me what was going on. I flipped open the Bible and read 'My grace is sufficient for you, for my power is made perfect in weakness' (2 Corinthians 12:9). Then it said, 'Therefore I will boast all the more gladly about my weaknesses, so that Christ's power may rest on me'. I promised God then and there that I would speak for him in public whenever I was asked, and I never went back on this promise. I did not really expect anyone to ask me to speak in public again, but later events were to prove how wrong I was. But throughout my Christian life, every time I stand up to speak I remember my verse, cast myself on him and begin. I have spoken in the Royal Albert Hall in London, on a soap box in Hyde Park, to a large Christian audience in the United Nations building in Nairobi, in St Paul's Cathedral, London, and in multitudinous smaller places.

It is no wonder that I called this book *Can it be me?* I have done many things for God as he opened them up, and spoken in public many times, but I have always known I was only his humble and grateful instrument. It certainly has been me who committed myself to God and began to do what he asked. But I recognised from the beginning that I could only do this because of the power he gave me. People sometimes feel that a statement such as this merely indicates a basic inferiority and lack of self respect, but that is not true. It means that we know he died for us because he thought we were important individuals, and his empowerment indicates that we have a God-given role to fulfil during our time on earth. One of my favourite translations of 1 Peter 5:7 reads 'It matters to him about you'. Another version reads 'He cares for you affectionately, and cares about you watchfully' (The Amplified New Testament, Zondervan). In my context, it matters to him that I need power to speak in public, power to serve him in the many different things he has asked me to do for him, power to keep praying and reading the Bible when it is so easy to neglect them, and power to keep my sense of humour and remain an ordinary human being, not a work machine. This, incidentally, has taken me many years to learn! All this Peter sums up very clearly in his first letter, chapter 4:11: 'If anyone serves, he should do it with the strength God provides, so that in all things God may be praised through Jesus Christ'.

Time rolled by. I passed my second professional examination, and was now ready to start working in hospitals. This meant leaving Exeter and embarking on the very varied clinical training that my excellent medical school had organised, despite the problems created by the war. I began in a place called Arlesey where an emergency hospital had been set up in the grounds of a large old fashioned mental hospital. Our first course was in Pathology, followed by medical and surgical posts. We had

Shardeloes, a stately home, became a wartime midwifery hospital

very good tuition, and I loved it all. My sister had also been to Arlesey and later got a distinguished award to do an extra year in pathology there, but sadly I had moved on to my next posting by that time. I was able to take over her student lodgings, living with a lovely lady who belonged to the Plymouth Brethren. I went with her to their services and to the young peoples' meetings on a Saturday evening. They were wonderful Bible teachers, but in that generation were also very strict. Women could not speak, they had to have long hair, always wear a hat in church, and a lot of other rules and regulations. Due to my background and personality structure, these restrictions plus those traditionally current in the IVF at the time were not really very good for me, and it took several years and a major personal upheaval to enable me to move into the freedom the Lord wanted for me.

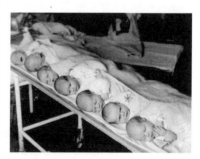

We delivered a lot of babies in 24 hours!

Because of the war many hospitals had moved to the country, so after a year at Arlesey I began rotating to all sorts of places for different study modules. We had a red card that had to be ticked off by the head of each department, and if it was not done then you could not sit the final exams. For example, I did obstetrics in a stately home in

Amersham, the historic long gallery being the lying-in ward after delivery, and the labour ward the old servants' quarters. It was all great fun. I did paediatrics in London and Carshalton, helped in casualty at the Royal Free Hospital, our alma mater, then back to Arlesey, and finally entered the last stretch. I passed all my exams first time apart from medicine where I made a mistake in the clinical exam, but was able to pass it three months later. After I got my results I had arranged to meet my mother in the heart of London, and when I came up from the Underground into Oxford Circus all the flags had come out. For a fleeting moment I thought it was for

The old Royal Free Hospital, where we learned clinical skills

me, the new doctor! In reality it was to signal the end of the war in Europe, so my mother and I went straight down to Buckingham Palace, cheered the King, Queen and Princesses on the balcony, and afterwards went off for a lovely celebration meal.

I then had to begin my junior doctor house jobs, as they were called in those days. If you wanted to work with a particular doctor you had to stand in the quadrangle in the Royal Free Hospital, and when your target arrived you politely opened the car door and said you were applying for their house job. I duly followed the ritual and was appointed junior houseman in obstetrics and gynaecology. This was important to me, for by now I was starting to work out just what God wanted me to do with my life. I had remained active in the IVF (now UCCF), serving a period on the London branch committee after which I was invited to serve on the UK committee. This was another occasion when I asked myself 'Can it be me?' I still stammered, was improving in relationships, was reasonably good at my work, but still felt somewhat insecure. So when I was asked to help at senior committee level I was truly amazed that God could make me useful in this type of work. One thing that really helped me was the discovery that I had inherited the family gift of being able to talk easily with strangers. This was very useful when dealing with the many patients I saw, and also when caring for new students at Christian conferences.

It was not until I had completed two years' house jobs that I discovered God's will for my future life. I read a book by a famous woman doctor called Mary Scharleib. She had lived in India with her businessman husband. Because she was a woman she was often asked by secluded Muslim women to help them medically. These women lived in a separate area of the home called the Zenana. They were not allowed to see any men apart from their husbands and family, so if they were ill many felt they would rather die than break the rule and see a male doctor. And in Mary Scharleib's day many did die. As she tried to help she realised it was essential to be medically trained, but in those days women doctors were a rarity. A few had emerged from Germany and Scotland, and they saw the need to create a medical school for training women doctors. Against great opposition, the London School of Medicine for Women was founded and the senior staff persuaded the Royal Free Hospital to take their students for clinical experience, so that they could qualify officially. In reality there were many people who wanted women doctors, but it took several more years before they were appointed to senior roles in hospitals. Mary Scharleib was one of the earliest women to graduate and finally ended up as a senior consultant who once examined my mother! She played a leading role in the development of a group of very senior doctors who were interested in improving the health of serving missionaries. Perhaps the most useful thing was their regular monthly meeting, and the interest of this group of very well known specialists led to great improvements in missionary health care. They kept minutes, which make fascinating reading for those interested in mission history.

Returning to the Zenana work, by the mid 1800s Queen Victoria had got involved with the medical needs of secluded women due to an Indian Queen sending her a locket and asking her to do something to help. Victoria backed the founding of the Church of England Zenana Missionary Society (CEZMS), which was followed by the setting up of the interdenominational Zenana

Bible and Medical Mission (ZBMM). I heard the story and it really gripped me, so I decided to write to ZBMM for some literature. I had heard of a very special place in India called Benares, and discovered an article about it in the magazine they sent me. I opened it immediately, and at the top of the page were the words: 'Behold, I have set before thee an open door, and no man can shut it' (Rev 3:8 KJV). I knew immediately that I should explore the possibility of this being my 'unshuttable' open door, for I also knew that there would be obstacles. I first talked it over with my family and, as they were in agreement, I went ahead.

When I began to correspond with ZBMM I was invited to come to their headquarters and meet the office staff. It was like another world. The office was in a lovely old house in Surrey Street off the Strand in London. It went up and up for about five floors with rooms on every floor. I delayed ringing the bell for ages as the sign on the door said 'Normal Females Educational Establishment'. I knew I was female, but was I normal, and did I need to do even more about my education than I was already doing? I wandered on hoping to find ZBMM but the number on the Normal Females house was quite clear – it was definitely 33 Surrey Street, so I rang the bell. I later realised that the name was the original one given to the mission that later became the ZBMM, 'normal' indicating a pattern of female education. For several more years the mission cablegram address was 'Normal', much to our amusement. The door was opened by a small elderly man who asked me in, and when we had talked for a bit he set me off on a long journey upstairs. Long is the right word to use, for on every floor someone popped out to talk to me before sending me to the next person. They were all very nice, very well informed about India, most were elderly, and they were predominantly single women. At the end someone said I should go to the top floor and meet a lady there, and added with awe and respect that she was the author of a book called *But if Not*. I did not like to tell her I had never heard of it! The author turned out to be just like a wise little bird, younger than the rest of them and even smaller than I was. Because she had lived and worked in India she was very helpful, and could answer a lot of my questions.

After our conversation I was given a cup of tea and invited to the monthly meeting downstairs in the basement. This was a microcosm of pure Victoriana. Everyone but me wore a hat, they were all very elderly, there was an ancient harmonium, and everything was in rather Victorian language. But despite the generational gap I realised they were people who really prayed and believed, and had committed their time and much of their lives to prayer support and fundraising for the ZBMM. At the end the elderly gentleman said they would be in touch, gave me some literature and an application form, and I returned to the streets of 20th century post-war London.

One day I was asked to go to the office again to meet the elderly gentleman, who was, I discovered, the Administrative Secretary of the Mission. He told me the committee had read my application but had received an adverse reference from the church I attended when I was not out of London or tied up in the hospital. The pastor had written that I 'should never be sent to India because I was a very nervous person'. I knew why he had said this. I once asked him a spiritual question about something that was rather upsetting. I had been up all night anyway on a difficult obstetric case so was not feeling too good, and halfway through I forgot what we were supposed to be talking about. I needed some sleep! Presumably he based his comment on that meeting. I discussed it with the Secretary, and said I would leave it to them to decide if they wanted me or not. He then asked if I would be willing to have some preliminary missionary training if they decided to accept me, and I said 'Certainly'.

Some weeks later the Secretary wrote and said the Committee had accepted me, and would I let him know when I could start training. They suggested a year at Mount Hermon Missionary Training College, based in West London. It would be residential and have three terms with a break between each. No funds were provided for our personal expenses, I would have to 'live by faith' for those, but they would pay the fees. By that time I was doing a senior house job in Nottingham, and was committed there till July 1947, so I agreed to start at Mount Hermon in October 1947. One of the best consultants in the Nottingham hospital was very annoyed as he had his eye on me for a senior position in his unit, but after thanking him I explained I really felt God wanted me to go to India, so that was that. I learned later that another man I knew there had a rather different sort of eye upon me, but had never done much about it, and anyway, although I liked him as a friend, I would not have been interested in anything more.

After my very busy house jobs I was glad of a month off, during which my sister got married to Dr Peter Fraser. I had the pleasure of being her bridesmaid. She nearly did not get to her wedding. We had been asked to be punctual as there was another wedding straight after ours. The second lot were very 'upper crust', and wanted to take all our flowers out and put in their own specially designed décor. This was perfectly okay but it did mean we had to start our wedding on time. I went over to the church with the other bridesmaid, but Vicky never turned up. The poor rector was getting very agitated by the time she came. Apparently she had been unable to get the lift down from the fifth floor. It kept whizzing past, and in a bridal gown she could not walk down five flights of stairs. But all ended well and we had a lovely wedding.

When she went away on honeymoon, I had a short holiday and then set off for the first part of my missionary training, my second steep learning curve after being a medical student. For me this was a totally blind date. I had never met anyone who had been to a missionary training college, and had been a bit startled by the clothes requirements. I was to find a long-sleeved navy blue dress with a neck that could take a collar. There were several other things, but they said the hats and badges would be obtainable on arrival. I looked everywhere for the dress. In immediate post-war London we still had clothing coupons, but if you were pregnant you got clothes for fewer coupons. My search in the non-pregnant world did not reveal even one long-sleeved navy blue dress, so I turned to the maternity department where I found just one. It seemed to fit me okay and there would be no need for me to expand it because I was not, of course, pregnant, but they let me have it for the reduced number of coupons when I told them I was going to India.

So armed with my maternity dress I set off for Mount Hermon in Ealing, West London, where I discovered the meaning of the collar requirement in our dress information. They provided stiff starched collars which we had to stitch on, and change twice a week. We wore this uniform the whole time plus a weekday hat like a pork pie, and a Sunday hat. The setup was very much like a boarding school, with a lot of rules and regulations, but the whole atmosphere was pleasant despite being a bit strict. I discovered that for two thirds of the whole year we had to keep a record of how we spent our time from 6 am to 8 pm five days a week. This had to be entered into a sort of account book, added up weekly and submitted to the principal. There was also a column for the time you took doing your timetable, and due to my poor arithmetic skills this tended to be rather a large amount of Friday time. Going to the toilet was classed as recreation!

Mount Hermon was housed in a very nice property in a lovely road. It was known as one of the best training colleges available at that time, despite being somewhat old fashioned, and a few years later joined with three other colleges to found the famous All Nations Christian College. Lectures on doctrine were very good, the Bible studies interesting but not really academically oriented. We learned a lot of practical things such as book-keeping and cooking, but there was very little on cross-cultural living which was not really discussed anywhere in those days. We did, however, learn a lot about prayer, world need, and the importance of caring for our spiritual lives during our future service. In the vacations I was able to do locums in a general practice I had worked in before starting my house jobs, and this kept me in touch with medical practice throughout my time at Mount Hermon, as well as giving me a bit of money.

The students did all the housework and this was on a rota system. In my first term I found I was appointed to cut bread and butter for breakfast, and then understood why I had been asked to bring an apron. As I had no more clothes coupons I brought my three hospital white coats. It was indeed a strange experience to be cutting bread and butter in the clothes I had worn on the wards, and I shed a few tears of longing to be back in hospital. But I knew I was doing the right thing so turned to finding ways of enjoying it.

The best thing was meeting and working with the other students. They came from all over the UK, and a few had been able to come from other countries. We had a lovely Dutch girl who was half starved during the war and still had plenty of oedema (swollen legs) to show for it. We fed and nurtured her, and found her a blessing to be with. Nothing that happened in Holland had caused her to deviate from her Christian belief. Another student was a special protégée of the Principal. She was a German Jewish Christian who had gone to Israel in one of the very early ships that had suddenly arrived there after the war. I never knew how she came to be at Mount Herman, but it was wonderful to have her. One of the people we all loved was a farm girl from Eastern England. She was physically very strong, and I once saw her lift a big iron stove out of the way in a garage. But she was indeed a gentle giant, a lovely-natured person, full of the Lord's grace, and she went on to make a great contribution to India.

Another special friend had got engaged to the son of a well-known UK evangelist and, as he was going to do the same as his father, she felt she should have some training before they married and began working together. I am grateful that although Mount Hermon was very old-fashioned compared with modern missionary training, it provided me with enduring friendships as well as experience of doing all sorts of new things, and the opportunity of thinking carefully about my beliefs and my future missionary service.

At the end of the first year I felt half-cooked. I realised I needed another year's experience of living and working with all sorts of people, and decided to ask ZBMM if I could do the second year. I also decided I needed to keep up with my profession, and arranged with Mount Hermon that I could be released for certain periods of time to study for a Diploma in Obstetrics. I attended the antenatal clinic in my old hospital once a week, and read my textbooks in the evenings, rules about going to bed being suspended for this one term. I sat the written papers and in the clinical exam experienced a God-given situation! I was asked to examine a pregnant lady, made a diagnosis and then met the examiner. When I told him what I had found he said, 'Oh no, sorry. You have got it wrong'. I asked him to examine her himself – and sure enough I was right. The baby had been a 'breech', upside down, but in the night had suddenly got tired of head up and decided to go head down, just in time for my examination. The abnormality was now a 'high head' pregnancy, and the examiner had not prepared questions for this. So we just talked about management. As we talked I mentioned that something which was always taught really did not seem to work, so either I was doing it wrong or it was not as good as it was supposed to be. We had an interesting discussion, and parted good friends. A few days later I got the news that I had passed, added DObst RCOG to my name, and went back to regular student life and preparing to go to India in 1949.

At this point a major problem emerged. There was no air travel so the only way to go to other countries was by sea. There was a crucial shortage of passenger ships due to massive sinking by torpedoes, as well as the need to convert troop ships back to passenger ships. Many missionaries had been waiting a long time to get to their new locations. At a conference in May 1949 we decided to have a night of prayer about this. We began to pray around 8 pm and prayed our hearts out till 2.30 am. Then we all stopped praying. We felt the work was done and that God was going to provide the ships – so sensibly had a nice cup of tea and went to bed. Within six months the back-log was cleared, and I had a date to sail to India on the P&O ship 'Corfu' on 21 October 1949.

# 3

# Life in the Indian subcontinent

Before the days of air travel the departure of the India and Far Eastern Boat Train from Victoria Station, London, was a big event. Every missionary society sending people overseas had representatives on the platform. The Salvation Army had a brass band, all the musicians getting red in the face as they tried to be heard over the general uproar. There were hymns and prayers all over the place. My family were there as well as mission representatives, and everyone kept pushing gifts into my hands. I had an orchid that lasted till we got into the Mediterranean, chocolates, papers, books and, for some strange reason, someone I hardly knew gave

The farewell at Victoria Station, London
My mother, sister in law and a friend

me the doll that had been on the top of her Christmas tree. It was rather large, and I did not quite know what to do with it, so on the train I gave it to a rather unhappy looking little girl. When the train guard began to blow his whistle as a sign that we should get on the train, there was a positive orgy of hugging and kissing, many tears, and so we were off. My sister had been unable to come due to having a young baby, Malcolm, so she told me to look out at a station called Berrylands where she would be right at the end of the platform waving a nappy. There she was, I waved frantically from the window, and we shouted goodbye.

The reason for all this fuss was that we were going away for a long time. It took about 16 days to get to India by sea, and travelling was expensive, so unless there was some dire emergency, the appointed period before we came home on leave was five years. We were all very conscious that it was to be a really long separation. When we finally arrived at Southampton docks and clambered out of the train, we saw the ship looming up before us. I said to myself 'Marjory, what *have* you done?' But there was no turning back at that point. When we got on board we found that the ship had been

Final discussion with Dr Mary Stokes

a troop carrier in the war, and had only recently been re-converted back into passenger status. Four of us shared a cabin, two berths up and two down, and this was situated right at the back end of the bottom deck, if you forgive my non-nautical English. It looked very nice, and there were more flowers and telegrams from our friends. Soon after we sailed the bell rang for dinner, and our spirits suddenly lifted when we saw the menu. What food! Half of it we had not been able to get in the war, and to eat bananas, wonderful desserts like chocolate puddings, plentiful roast meat or vegetarian foods was a wonderful treat after UK rationing.

Next morning our troubles began. The cabin, despite the traditional air-blower, was very hot, and we had been going up and down like yo-yos all night, with a nasty lurch in the middle of every up and down, the dreaded roll. The cabin steward brought us some tea and said, 'Are you crying yet? Everyone who has this cabin usually ends up crying'. But I did not stay to hear more, having to make a dash for the bathroom from which I emerged decidedly green in the face. So I decided to get out of the cabin, wrap up warm, find a chair in a sheltered place on deck, borrow a blanket and just stay there. We were now in the Bay of Biscay which could be very rough in late October, so I stayed on deck for two days just drinking a little tea and only going inside at night to sleep.

The third morning we woke to a totally new scene, Gibraltar, the blue of the Mediterranean ahead of us, sun and lovely calm seas. We emerged pale-faced, blinking in the sun, and began to relax. There was only a small group of missionaries on board but we got to know each other in a regular

Beyond the Bay of Biscay, a little bit of heaven

evening meeting, met a lot of very nice people among the non-missionary group, relaxed, swam, ate, prayed, read library books and said repeatedly to each other, 'This is the life! Who wouldn't be a foreign missionary?' Actually it was just what we all needed. We had been through the war where danger was ever present, and food got less and less and of poorer quality. Some had served in the Armed Forces themselves or manned the dangerous Volunteer posts, and we had not been able to relax due to our duties or anxieties about relatives fighting in the war. Consequently we were both under-nourished and over-tired, but now we had a chance to make up for it. We took the chance with both hands, and enjoyed life.

Our first stop was Port Said, the Western end of the Suez Canal. We did all the usual tourist sights, fighting off the 'gully gully men', and avoiding the traders whose usual call to attract our attention was 'Mrs Simpson, Mrs Simpson'. She was the divorced American woman with whom our proposed King Edward VIII fell in love before his coronation, and because of whom he decided to abdicate and give the throne to his brother, the future George VI. Why the Port Said traders used her name as a call signal I never found out.

The journey through the Suez Canal was a dream. We sat in the sun by the rails and watched the life of Egypt go by. On the other side we looked over the Sinai area and had plenty of sympathy for Moses and the children of Israel wandering in that desert land. As for us, tea time came, and waiters brought us tea, scones and cakes. As we said, we 'sat there like Lord and Lady Muck', an English joke for unaccustomed luxury, watching the Suez and Egypt go by.

When evening came I saw something I can never forget. We sat down to dinner by a glassed-over porthole, and I looked out to see a ship sailing by in the middle of the desert. I asked the steward what it was and he explained it was the new alternative canal, built so that in one small area there could be two-way traffic. It felt positively bizarre, eating dinner and watching 'the other lane' which was hidden from view apart from the upper parts of the ships moving through.

At the Eastern end we stopped at Suez itself, went ashore briefly, then back for the last lap across the Indian Ocean towards Bombay (now Mumbai). The end was in sight, viewed by me with a grand mixture of expectation and alarm. We docked about 4 am and I was awoken by a huge noise of people yelling and shouting. Remembering that since partition into India and Pakistan there had been heavy fighting between the people staying in India and those going over to live in Pakistan, I thought a massacre was going on, and the next cry would be 'murder the missionaries'. In reality, as a seasoned traveller told me, this was the habitual noise of Bombay docks.

When we disembarked I experienced my first miracle. I had been asked to bring with me some new surgical instruments for the hospital, and it was not until I read the customs regulations that I realised I could have to pay heavy duty. My cash in hand was just under ten pounds. My bank manager in London nearly had a heart attack when I told him I was going to take ten pounds out of my account before going to India, leaving the remaining three pounds to keep the account open while I was away. He took off his glasses, put them down with a slow and careful hand and said to me, 'Doctor are you telling me you are going to India with only ten pounds?' 'Yes' I said, 'and I am sure God will look after me as it is where he wants me to go'. From that moment the bank was exceedingly kind to me, taking care of my small income as if it was a fortune. I am still with the same branch sixty years later.

So there I was, on the docks, waiting to go through customs, with no money to pay duty on the badly needed instruments. I remembered a story in the Bible where God blinded the eyes of people who could cause trouble for the Israelites, and I prayed that he would blind the eyes of the customs officer to the instruments whose value I had declared honestly on the papers I submitted. He read my documents carefully and said 'no duty', so I hopped it as fast as I could, thanking God for the temporary attack of 'blindness' that had enabled me to get the instruments through.

From the docks we were taken to the Queen Mary High School, one of our mission projects. This was my first introduction to bungalow life, i.e. living with a community of single women in one house. They were all lovely people, and doing a great job, but it was very formal. At the end of dinner finger bowls were produced. I had read about these but never seen one, and I thought 'Cheers, we are going to have a lovely dessert'. Instead, one boiled sweet wrapped in paper was handed out to each of us, and as they were sticky in the heat we washed our fingers in the finger bowl. No mangoes or other exotica! Then to bed under a mosquito net, a very comfortable experience under a slowly turning fan, up for a very small breakfast and then to the station to get the train. I was to go to Lucknow where I was appointed to the staff of the Lady Kinnaird Hospital, a long-established women's hospital colloquially known as the Douglas Hospital after a very famous medical superintendent.

When we reached Bombay's magnificent Victoria station I discovered I was travelling with a man I had met on the ship. He was connected with a well-known mission in UK, and had been asked to make pastoral visits to all their work, starting with Lucknow. We shared a two-berth first class cabin, and set off with great excitement on our journey through West India to Lucknow in the North. I have decided to be honest in this book, and therefore must write about my companion. He fell in love with me on the ship, a classical, and often despised, 'ship board romance'. No wonder. The moon over the Red Sea, with dance music coming down from the first class, was a very romantic experience. I was not at all sure what I felt about him. At that time, to marry him would have meant leaving ZBMM, which, due to the specialised nature of its work, sent out only women missionaries. The long journey gave us a chance to talk, and I was able to start sorting out my own mind. To finish this story here, I finally decided not to marry him. I have always been grateful to God that he enabled me to see clearly that I should not consider marriage at that time, and indeed should be willing to remain single if that was what I called his 'first best will' for me. Of course many single missionaries did marry, but this was not to be the route God had in mind for me. As I have often said, I am sure I would have been a dreadful wife and mother, but would have made a marvellous grandmother. Thankfully I have two great-nieces who enable me to fulfil that role, but I have never dared ask them if I am a marvellous great aunt or not!

Twenty eight hours later we arrived in Lucknow in the late evening. The annual riots between the Shia and Sunni communities

The Kinnaird Hospital bungalow in which most of the missionaries lived

were taking place in the city, and a curfew had been imposed. The staff had to get a police permit to come and meet me at the station and, after saying goodbye to my friend, I was whisked off in the hospital car. On arrival it was pitch dark but I was aware of a nice large bedroom with a mosquito net, a comfortable desk and chair, and an attached bathroom. So I dropped into bed, learned how to tuck in the net and was instantly asleep.

Next morning I was woken at 6.30 am by a man with a tray of *chota hazri*, the 'little breakfast'. This was tea, toast, a little jam and a very small banana. After that I got up, dressed, prayed and went out on the verandah outside my room. I was living in a huge bungalow, built in traditional British Raj style (Raj meant kingdom, or rule, and was the term applied to anything connected with the

British occupation). There was a wonderful garden full of strange trees, masses of unfamiliar birds, and a few Indian men wandering about looking after things. They all said 'Salaam' as they passed me and I could only smile. I then went to morning prayers and saw the hospital. This was a large typical style building on three sides of a large square, the centre being occupied by a lovely garden. The setup seemed a little primitive in some ways, and much of the equipment looked out of date. There was no intravenous drip facility so no blood or saline transfusions were possible. Laboratory work was very limited. But everything was very well cared for and the patients looked happy. The senior doctor, Dr Hodge, had been born in India, spoke marvellous Urdu and was a very good surgeon. There were three excellent Indian doctors. No one had higher qualifications, i.e. postgraduate specialty degrees, but we all did many of the things that only specialists would do in the UK.

I wondered why the bedsteads were made of iron until I sat down on one to look at a baby, and in a few minutes I knew why. I began itching all over, and discovered I was a very popular target for bedbugs. These were the curse of the hospital, and every three months all the metal bedsteads had alcohol poured over them and were set alight. This solved the problem for a few weeks but then the bugs were back. I remained a prime target the rest of my Indian career – they just loved me. In fact it became a standing joke when the bugs got too bad: 'Ask Marjory to come and sit on the bed for a bit, that will solve the problem!'

After this preliminary trot round, I went back to the bungalow and discussed my programme. Initially language study would be the primary thing, although I would do a little work in the hospital as well. Meanwhile, as an emergency, would I be willing to be on call if a private patient of the senior doctor went into labour. She herself would be tied up with a mission administration conference. When the call came I had my first experience of childbirth in an Indian hospital, managing the case with the only Hindi word they taught me, the one for 'push'.

The next few months were a mixture of bewilderment, frustration and enjoyment. I discovered this was a wonderful time to be in India. They had been independent of the British for two years, the massacres between the Hindu and Muslim groups were over, and the country was settling down to independent democracy. Pandit Nehru, one of the great pioneers in the freedom struggle, was Prime Minister, and Dr Rajendra Prasad, another famous freedom leader, was the President of the Republic. The whole country was buzzing with excitement and new hope. Pandit Nehru lived in New Delhi, but travelled to other areas of India very frequently. I saw him several times, usually with his daughter, Indira Gandhi, who later also became Prime Minister until she was murdered by her bodyguards. There were exhibitions of Five Year Plans, and the atmosphere was full of enterprise and energy. It was a grand experience. It also provided us with an opportunity to get over to the people what we had been telling them for 100 years. They had never really believed we missionaries were not connected to the Raj, the

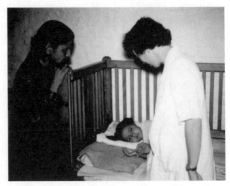

Typical ward round scene, Kinnaird Hospital

British ruling power, and when they discovered we had not left with the Raj people and proposed staying on indefinitely, they began to understand we were nothing to do with Government but everything to do with Jesus Christ.

While all this excitement was going on in the country, I was struggling with learning Hindi. As soon as my classes began

Village patients waiting to be seen

I realised there was one problem area we had never considered when I made my application. I discovered I had to learn two languages, Hindi first, at basic and higher level, two examinations being involved, followed by Urdu, the *lingua franca* for many of our patients. What I had not realised was that we learned the language by first mastering Hindi phonetics and script and then reading words and sentences aloud – and of course my big problem was inability to read aloud! In addition I had to take my turn reading the Bible passage for the day at lunchtime prayers. So I sat down in my bedroom and considered my position. I took hold in faith of the words God had given me so many years ago. 2 Corinthians 12:9 says, 'My grace is sufficient for you, for my power is made perfect in weakness'. And sitting in my new room in Lucknow, facing the horrors of learning a language by reading aloud, I responded in faith with the other half of the same verse, 'I will boast all the more gladly about my weaknesses, so that Christ's power may rest on me….for when I am weak I am strong'. I rededicated myself to God and to language learning, thrown completely on his power for it all. To finish part of this story here, I never did master reading aloud, but in my later career this helped me, for I was forced to lecture in ordinary colloquial English from very basic notes, which made a flowing and fresh approach to my material rather than just reading aloud a prepared lecture. I also learned by heart any Bible verses I wanted to quote, since I had no trouble at all in repeating learned material, and this was very good for my soul.

During this period I was also learning a little about how India and the mission setup worked, visiting famous places in Lucknow, feeling hugely homesick, and finding the bungalow routine rather heavy going. The Western missionaries lived together in the bungalow and a few other nearby rooms outside the locked door to the hospital. As was the traditional pattern the Indian staff lived within the hospital area. I grew accustomed to the vagaries of Indian locks, and later on I made it my annual duty to oil every lock in the hospital in which I was currently working. Bungalow life followed a set routine, and because we all lived together we had little or no private life. We could make tea in our own rooms but that was about all. We had little opportunity to make or entertain private friends from the Western or Indian communities. This was not abnormal – it was the missionary custom in Lucknow during the Raj period and it had not yet modernised itself. On the whole I just took it in my stride, but it was not very good for me. As I have said earlier, although I was much improved I still

The staff of Kinnaird Hospital
The famous Dr Douglas (2nd from right, front row) was visiting us

had problems mixing socially and bungalow life on this pattern only compounded the problem. An added difficulty was that I got amoebic and bacillary dysentery very early on in my Indian career and this made eating Indian food difficult – but I persevered and tried to like it.

After six months in Lucknow I went to the hills to attend Language School. We lived at an altitude of about 6500 feet in a place called Landour, where there was a language school and a good hospital serving both missionaries and the local population. Our house was perched on the edge of a hill looking over a wide expanse of the Indian plains, and I loved it. Language school began with

Language school –
Marjory keeping her nose to the grindstone

the Principal thanking us all for coming, but he then explained that by doing so we had merely added to the number of India's illiterates. We could not read, write or speak! This was very good for us, making us realise that our past academic achievements would be useless unless we could communicate. We went to school in the mornings, and in the afternoons had our own private tutor plus private study. My problem became enormous. I not only had difficulty in reading aloud, and the whole course consisted of that, but I had learned very little English grammar – it was out of fashion when I was educated. I was blessed by having the best teacher in the school and one day he put the books down and said sadly, 'If you don't know any English grammar how can I teach you Hindi grammar?' So I apologised to him, and said I would try very hard to catch up on my deficiencies. He was very kind and patient with me over my speech problem, and discovered I did much better if I tried conversation, or used material I had previously learned by heart such as the dreaded 'model sentences' in Hindi. We had nearly 200 of these to learn, and most of us put them on small cards and threaded them up with string like a gigantic rosary. Many of us could be seen wandering round the hill paths turning over our 'rosary' and muttering to ourselves. One sentence was 'I have to

Typical language school scene
Note the (then) mandatory topee!

give you two or three annas', Indian currency still being rupees and annas. My moment of glory came when I really did owe the office three annas for a postage stamp so I went in, reeled off my model sentence and felt fine!

Things came to a climax when I discovered that not only did I stammer but I also had several very abnormal phonetics in my speech. In Hindi there are two different ways of saying the sound 'ch' as in 'church', and two more for 'j'. Since I could not say them properly in English things were starting to look grim, and I began to get disheartened and anxious. I decided to go and have a talk with the American lady acting as language advisor to the students. She was a woman who really believed in prayer, and after we had talked and I had had a good weep, she said, 'Why don't we pray?' So we knelt down and began to ask God to help me to do the work for which he had sent me to India. Then she said to me, 'Put your tongue like this in your mouth', demonstrating in her own mouth how to do it, 'and then say "ch".' So I did, and she said excitedly 'That's it'. I heard the difference myself. Then I did 'chh' and both the 'js' and started work on a few other sounds as well. I was so thankful and excited, and spent the next few days listening to every word I said in English and changing the abnormal 'ch' and ' j' and 'r' into the new ones I had learned. I began practising them in Hindi, and when I went to my teacher for my next lesson he was very pleased to hear me so much better. I told him how God had really helped me, and we had a fine talk. Forty years later when I was travelling in Pakistan someone said to me 'Where did you learn such beautiful Urdu?', the second language I learned which had some of the same phonetics as Hindi. I felt that was real proof of how God had moved in on my language problem, for Pakistan is the home of common speech Urdu, although Lucknow was the home of classically beautiful Urdu. Even today when I meet Urdu speakers on the London Underground they exclaim 'What beautiful Urdu you speak'.

Regretfully I had to leave Landour early due to a crisis in another of our hospitals. This one was in Patna, Bihar, right on the edges of the Ganges. I was asked to go there to help out, continuing language with a local teacher while working in the hospital. Patna was much less formal, with a relaxed atmosphere, and the hospital was better equipped although still lacking in many modern necessities due to lack of funds. The senior doctor was Win (Sandy) Anderson, and the evangelist and general pastoral carer was her great friend Win Emery. They were very good to me, and I loved them dearly. We worked very hard but used to go out into the countryside to relax, have a picnic, and give out Christian booklets to people we met on the way. I continued language study and took and passed both my Hindi language exams in Patna after a second short period in Landour. Sandy went home on leave and I was asked to be in charge, assisted by a venerable missionary doctor called Kitty Harbord who deserves a book of her own. She came from a very upper crust diplomatic family, and had a sudden conversion to faith in Jesus Christ just before the usual annual visit to Ascot races, a very smart occasion indeed. She told her father she could only come if she could bring her Christian booklets with her and give them away. The thought of her doing that in the Royal Enclosure was more than her father could take, so he agreed she should stay at home. After serving in India for some time she became ill with cancer, and after surgery in the UK was one of the first patients to be treated with radium. They did not get the dose right and she developed an ulcer which never healed until her final years in India as a very old lady. Some years before I met her she had been asked to go into the then closed country of Nepal to deliver the daughter of the Governor of a small city called Tansen, where I worked some years later. She could not walk all the way so was carried up in a kind of box called a doolie. It was so small that it put severe pressure on her toenails and, after a short time, they all turned black and dropped off by the time she arrived.

Before Sandy went away on home leave I had a curious experience which was to influence the rest of my life. It is not easy for me to write about this, but my story would be incomplete if I did not do so. We had a visiting itinerant Indian Christian preacher who went round churches holding special meetings. (He later married a doctor who worked to support him so that he could be free for his very effective ministry.) He asked people with any need or illness to come forward so that he and the team of helpers from the church could pray for them. I felt I needed to go forward for help with the remaining difficulties in my speech, but instead of praying for me in the church he asked me to come next day to the mission guest house where he was staying, accompanied by some friends, because he wanted to discuss the matter with me. I asked Sandy and Win to come with me and we all met in the bungalow of a local mission school. Having heard my story he asked me to kneel and began to pray. I do not know what happened after that, but some years later asked Sandy about it. Apparently I just dropped to the floor unconscious as soon as he began to pray that I would be freed from my speech problem. The next thing I knew Sandy and Win were supporting me and I was clutching the man's Indian style robe as if my life depended on it. He then anointed me with oil and we went away. I knew something had happened to me, I was not fully healed of my stammer, but I was different in some way I did not understand. As we went out a little boy I knew from the school came dashing up and climbed into my arms, and I felt as if God had blessed me with a new love and inner freedom that would serve me well in the future. I was aware that an inner spiritual healing had been involved, and began to study the Bible more intelligently, and to pray with more freedom for many people needing a similar touch from God. I still stammered, and remained the same old somewhat difficult me, but there was a new freedom in my life as well as a new commitment.

After Sandy left I was technically in charge, and so had to do a good deal of surgery, as well as abnormal midwifery, and a plethora of other types of medical care. The clinical experience was fabulous, and for the first time I also began treating missionaries and their families. We had patients with all kinds of tropical diseases as well as the usual ailments of women and children. I was glad that in Landour I had taken a course in microscopic examinations of various kinds, and so was familiar with the parasites that were such a common feature of medical practice in India. Later on I was to assist at an operation on a child of three years who had 355 roundworms impacted in her bowel. (I was responsible for counting them!!). Although my training was inadequate I learned how to do many forms of gynaecological surgery and I found the overall medical experience absolutely fascinating. I was also starting my Urdu studies, necessitated by the fact that this was the *lingua franca* of the large numbers of Muslim women who came to the hospital. I was just about to start learning the script when my teacher put out his tongue to show me how to pronounce something. 'Please, Master Sahib, will you put out your tongue again?' I said politely. He had a huge inoperable cancer on his tongue, so I advised him to see a doctor at once. But it was too late and he died within a few months. I never had time to learn the script but continued to speak Urdu better than pure Hindi, and was excused the exam due to my heavy medical work load.

When Sandy returned I went back to Lucknow, after a brief stay in the Western India ZBMM hospital at Nasik. For some reason our new Field Leader, a marvellous man called Alan Norrish, wanted to change the staffing of the three ZBMM hospitals, probably because he felt Lucknow was a very heavy load for me as a new missionary. So the doctor at Nasik was asked to come to Lucknow, where she spoke no language, and I was to go to Nasik where I spoke no language! Just before setting off I got a telegram to go as far as Allahabad, a famous city that one sees on TV these days during the Kumbh Mela, and wait there for instructions. After a few days I got a telegram from Alan: 'Feel Foyle and Divine aid adequate for situation, proceed Nasik', so off I went. Incidentally, many English people know the word 'doolali', an ex-Army word applied to mentally ill soldiers. This comes from a place near Nasik called Deolali, which was the holding station for mentally ill troops and others waiting for a ship to UK. The fact that I insert this here indicates my growing passion for both Indian and British history, which was to keep me going through a long and busy life, together with the other passion, birdwatching.

I only stayed at Nasik for ten days, it was obvious that it would be better if the old Nasik doctor and I changed places, so back I went to Lucknow as the 'in charge'. This role was one of the dying facets of mission life. In those days Western-based missions owned mission properties overseas – and often the land on which they stood. Much of the funding came from overseas, and an expatriate was almost always in charge. This has all changed now; ownership of mission projects is usually vested in the national church, and modern missionaries commonly work under the direction of one of the national staff, but in 1953 this had not yet occurred. As the only Western missionary doctor left in Lucknow, and the only one to have adequate qualifications, I had to be in charge, which was the last thing I wanted.

I was looking forward to going home on leave in 1954, but was so glad I was still in India to experience the changes that took place from 1952 onwards. We had a new ZBMM General Secretary in the UK, a highly skilled man called Jack Dain, later to become a Bishop in Australia. He was a wonderful friend to us all, and we benefited by his past experience. He had made the Navy his career, later became a missionary in North India and, at the outbreak of the second World War, volunteered to join a Gurkha regiment (mainly Nepali soldiers). After several eventful years he rejoined the Navy and had extensive experience of shore-based training of new personnel. His wife became ill and they had to return to London, where he was asked to stay on in London as Chief Staff Officer to the Royal Indian Navy. When he was free to leave the Navy in 1947, he was asked by ZBMM to become the first Field Leader, but finally, because of his wife's health, they could not go so he became the General Secretary in London. Alan and Sylvia Norrish joined us in India, one as Field Leader and the other as Manageress of the Edgehill Guest House near the Language School. Alan had a distinguished career in Malaysia during the war, serving in a Gurkha regiment. He spoke good Nepali and a little Hindi. He turned down an invitation to become a Minister in the new Malaysian Government in order to join us in ZBMM, mainly because he felt called by God to the job, but also because he and Jack were old friends and would make a good partnership. This led to a period of massive and very stimulating change. In 1953, we all agreed it was time to accept men into the mission, for in the new India, Bangladesh and Pakistan our role was changing, and expanding in many different directions. We then, of course, had to change our name. We stopped being the ZBMM ('The Bananas' as other missionaries called us), and formed The Bible and Medical Missionary Fellowship, or BMMF.

In the new India, and the other countries we were beginning to serve, the other major change was that the time had come to make the national Church leaders of Christian work – and Missions the servants of these Churches. Jack was a strategist, and one of the first questions he had asked in 1951 was why our annual prayer guide was mainly about missionaries. Why was there no mention of the local nationalised or indigenous churches? This was the beginning of a rethink of the role of missionaries, so that today we think of ourselves much more as servants of the church, enabled to go overseas by our missions, but not fully controlled by them. This was very stimulating, and boded well for our future development. Our final change some years later was to become

Going home the cabin was more comfortable

'Interserve', moving out of solely Asian ministry to a worldwide organisation, with national headquarters in many countries.

But I anticipate. Shortly after we became BMMF, I went to Bombay to go on my first home leave in May 1954. This time I was on the P&O ship *Himalaya*, larger than the first one, thank God, and we had a slightly better cabin. Once again life on board was marvellous. I was terribly tired, and had 16 wonderful days off-call, able to eat and sleep, to swim, and enjoy the lovely sunshine.

On arrival in London I went to live with my mother who had moved into another flat. The UK seemed rather strange and a lot had changed. For example, I rather unwisely went out alone and got on a bus. Having noticed a lot of orange globes blinking out a light at regular intervals by the roadside, I turned to the lady beside me and said, 'Excuse me, what are those orange lights?' She stared at me and said in a Cockney accent, 'Where yu bin living luv, the moon?' I explained about India and she told me about Belisha beacons, lights indicating where pedestrians could cross the road. I then tried a supermarket, a new development in the UK. There was so much choice I ran out of the shop with only a small bar of soap, terrified by the hyper-abundance of things available in post war Britain. I realised that after five solid years in India I was badly out of touch with things in my home country. My family were wonderful,

and when they realised how confused I was, they rallied round to help me. My sister-in-law Tess took me clothes shopping, Vicky and her family gave me a lot of love and care, my mother looked after me domestically and in other ways, and my brother took up my local and musical knowledge again. I was introduced to the delights of black and white TV and learned how to use a modern radio.

The only snag was the daunting programme of 'deputation work', a year-long round of speaking about BMMF work all over the UK. It was heavy work, but I began to enjoy it. I knew I would be speaking very frequently, and I still stammered, but I remembered my earlier promise to the Lord that I would speak for him whenever I was asked and he truly helped me. No one complained about my speech and the meetings progressed well. One day I made an important discovery. I arrived at a place in Cornwall, South West England. I was speaking at a women's meeting in a small church, and it was a real struggle from start to finish, due mainly to it being a very hot day and my own tiredness. I stammered fairly badly but managed to get through it. Immediately after the meeting a lady came up and said, 'I am so glad I heard you today. My daughter stammers, and says she can't do anything for anyone

A hat was mandatory for deputation work

and stays in her bedroom all day. I am going straight home to tell her about you, graduating, going to India, learning two languages, and serving the Lord there.' I felt so grateful, and decided that from then on I would trust the Lord with the outcome of my work, whether I stammered or not.

I finally came to enjoy deputation but there was one big snag. In those days no time was allocated for professional upgrading and development. I had missed out on clinical experience of the many new medicines that had recently come into use. I needed to know about things like antidepressants, tranquillisers, various forms of antibiotics and steroids, but nothing professional was woven into my furlough programme and it did not occur to me that it might be possible to change the old pattern. Another problem was not having enough money to buy new textbooks, attend professional conferences and take regular journals. My sister resolved the journal problem by sending me her copies by sea mail, but I missed regular professional discussion meetings and upgrades.

None of this was due to Mission carelessness. It was, I think, related to the old idea that medicine, or teaching, or any other similar professional activities were tools for evangelism rather than Christian service in their own right. I never agreed with this, for I was called to be a Christian doctor, which meant treating sick people, as well as helping them to understand something about the Lord I served.

At this point I want to affirm strongly that those in charge of us were absolutely wonderful people whom I admired immensely, and my problems do not imply any criticism. But things had changed since the war, and war time experiences had bred a different sort of young missionary. It took a little time for conditions and terms of service to catch up with the post-war generation and, as I indicated earlier, I was enormously proud of BMMF and the grand way we were being led by Jack, Alan and the committees at home and overseas. Much later on we were to experience the same thing again, the younger generations having new and radical ideas about how missions should work. So life is truly a series of circles, and what you learn first time round may prove very profitable later on.

# 4

# A big change

A few months before I was due to return overseas I was asked to come to the London office to discuss something. Jack Dain asked me if I would be interested in going to Nepal.

Many people had prayed for years for Nepal, which was closed to foreigners other than people like the British Army Gurkha officers who recruited there. The country had been taken over by a group called the Ranas, the King being a virtual prisoner. He managed to escape and fled to India, but after negotiation with the Ranas, and by popular demand, he returned as reigning monarch determined to set Nepal on the road to democracy. Soon after his return he received a rather odd petition from the people of Tansen, a small town in the hills of Western Nepal. A party of birdwatchers from the Natural History Museum, Chicago, USA, led by Dr Bob Fleming, had been allowed to go to the hills round Tansen to survey the bird population, which finally resulted in publication of a famous book on Birds of Nepal. Two couples went to stay in Tansen, and while half the party was birding, the other half, who were both doctors, opened a clinic for the local people. They were swamped with patients, treating locally as many as they could, and advising the rest to go to India. They began discussing with the locals whether or no they would appreciate a permanent hospital, which led to the petition to the King. When permission was granted the Flemings very wisely asked his consent to open hospitals in both Kathmandu and Tansen, realising that a base in the capital would be essential for the more isolated work to survive. This was accepted and so what became the United Mission to Nepal was born.

'United' was the important word, for from the start it was an inter-mission venture. Another group had already opened work in

Pokhra, now a very well known tourist spot, but they remained as an independent entity. When Jack asked me if I would be willing to go to Tansen, where I would be the first resident woman doctor in the whole area, I agreed without hesitation, and so began to prepare for another great adventure starting in October 1956.

Shanta Bhawan, an old palace, became the Kathmandu Hospital

It was decided that I should go first to Kathmandu, and after a week to get used to Nepal would then fly by the new air service to a place called Bhairawa where I would be met and escorted to Tansen. Kathmandu was wonderful. I remember sitting in the now famous Durbar Square and realising I was the only non-Nepali person there. No one hassled me, they were all doing their own thing, which included worshipping a huge idol of the goddess Kali, or coming to see the Kumari (princess). She was a little girl whom the people believed to be the reincarnation of a goddess, and periodically she came to an open window so that the people could see her. For the people this was a very holy appearance. Being the Kumari was not an easy life, because if she cut herself by accident, or began to menstruate, she immediately ceased to be the incarnate goddess and became an ordinary girl. Since no one really wanted to marry her, things were never easy for her again. But at the time I was there she was still appearing regularly at her window, and I just sat there and let Nepali life flow round me. I was very soon in love with the country and its delightful people. I understood then why Jack and Alan had felt so privileged to serve in Gurkha regiments.

The new UMN Hospital was in a palace, the much loved Shanta Bhawan. The Flemings had been delayed so it was in a holding position, staffed by an elderly Indian lady doctor and a nurse, who while awaiting arrival of the permanent staff held outpatient clinics. But the hospital in embryo was there, and in due time developed into a first class hospital. This later moved to a purpose-built hospital, half Government and half Mission funded. This was a very good setup, but to the oldies like me it never matched the exotic atmosphere of the old palace!

There were certainly some unusual places in the building. I asked to go to the toilet and was taken to a room tiled with alternating red and white tiles on every wall, floor and ceiling. I could not find the toilet anywhere, and had to ask for help. I discovered it was what we called a 'squatty potty', a Nepali-style toilet let into the floor, and the tiles had effectively camouflaged it. This was my first Nepali surprise and there were many more to come as I explored that wonderful country.

A week later I set off to Bhairawa. The Nepal air service in those days consisted of three small planes flown by foreign pilots from a variety of countries. The first two crashed, and I went off in the only remaining one. The pilot was drunk, and invited me into the cockpit. I decided if we were going to crash then the front

Tansen in 1955

47

might be better than the back, so I accepted the invitation and sat by him all the way, closing my eyes as we wobbled down. The next flight he was killed, so obviously God still had a bit more for me to do! One of the Tansen hospital staff, a very nice Swedish man called Ragnar Elfgaard, had been sent down to meet me, and we got on a rickety taxi that bumped over a rough road to Butwol, where we had a hospital agent. Having hired the necessary porters to carry our luggage we set off on our long walk. The first part of the trail ran through a high cliff

The hotels on the trail to Tansen

gorge beside a river, which was fine in the dry weather but became a raging torrent in the rainy season. There was no bridge so in the wet weather fishermen carried pedestrians over. At the end of the gorge was a gigantic stone staircase, made many years ago by slave labour. This went on for about four hours, so half way up we stopped for the night in a local inn. These inns were the brothels,

I arrive at Tansen for the first time

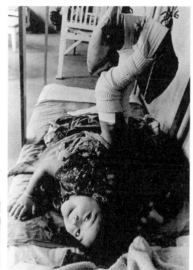

Local boys were trained for different work in the hospital

Tansen patient: 'I wish I had never climbed that tree to get firewood down'

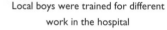

waiting to pounce on British Army Gurkha soldiers coming home with money in their pockets, but the women were always very kind to us and during my stay in Nepal I spent many nights alone in their back room while trade went on in the front.

Next morning I found my haversack had been robbed, but my passport was okay and that was all I really cared about. We went on up the trail, but by this time the hospital horse had arrived and I was invited to get on. Never having ridden a horse I was dead scared, and in fact only used it for one more journey. I preferred to walk! But this first time I climbed aboard, and on we went, along a flat plain, up another mountain, down again, along a plain, and finally a four hour climb up to Tansen. I was so stiff I had to be hauled off the horse like a sack of grain, and made my first entrance into the hospital with decidedly bandy legs.

Tansen Hospital was led by a marvellous pair, Dr Carl and Mrs Betty Anne Friedericks from the USA. He was a most enterprising man, and had already started to train some of the local boys to do blood and other laboratory tests, using a rather dilapidated microscope. Others were taught nursing skills, or were trained as operation assistants.

Carl's major interest was orthopaedics, which was a good thing, as one of the most frequent accidents was children falling out of trees while cutting firewood and breaking their legs. I soon learnt how to string them up on pulleys without always having to call Carl. He had got us a small second hand X-Ray machine from US army surplus, which was a godsend. Betty Anne, his wife, was wonderful. I have known many great missionary women and Betty Anne comes high on the list. She was beautiful and gifted,

The haunted house that we turned into Tansen Hospital

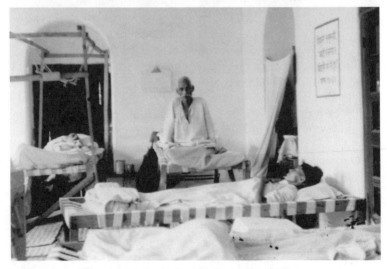

The men's ward, using local furniture and packing cases

and was dedicated to supporting her husband, caring for the children, one of whom was born in Tansen, and caring for all of us as well. I think everyone loved the Friedericks, and at the recent anniversary to celebrate 50 years of hospital work in Tansen, Carl and Betty Anne were seated in a big doolie and carried round the town on men's shoulders, to general acclaim.

The Elfgaards from Sweden were also fabulous people. She was a nurse and opened a regular antenatal clinic in the town, and he was in an administrative and pastoral role. We loved them and their children, one also born in Tansen.

The hospital was in a 'haunted house' in the centre of town. The people would not go near it before we took it over, but were willing to come if we were there because, as they told us, 'your God will protect us'. We all lived upstairs, the wards being on the ground floor. Beds were made of packing cases and boards with straw mattresses, and worked just fine.

I was to live with Ingeborg, a wonderful Norwegian nurse who is now a legend in UMN history. I was able to meet her a few months ago in Norway, both of us being 83 years old! She

Ingeborg and I very rarely quarrelled –
and then it was about food, Nepali,
Norwegian or UK style

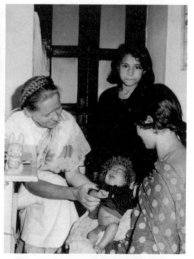

The much loved Ingeborg in her clinic

said something which really touched me. 'Marjory, when we lived together we had a lovely time didn't we, we never quarrelled except sometimes about food.' That was absolutely true, and I count it a great privilege to have shared with her, for she was not only a legend in Nepal but was awarded a medal by the King of Norway for her services. Using only what the women had in their poor houses, she developed a scheme for safer, cleaner, home delivery, so that they would have less infection after childbirth. She also gave simple training to the traditional midwives, outcaste women who inherited the job. Being from Norway she was a great walker, and would often go off on the difficult trails to try to help someone in complicated labour. If there was any possibility of saving them she would then get the patient carried in to see me at the hospital. She is one of the people I count it a privilege to have known.

We all settled down very happily. Inevitably we had our squabbles but they never lasted long, we apologised to each other, and absolutely revelled in our work. The medical work was fascinating. It was in some ways a raw population, for many people could not afford medical care and had never been exposed to antibiotics and other modern medicines. I was amazed at the way in which even cases with cavitation in the lungs from pulmonary tuberculosis cleared up on streptomycin, which had rarely been

Typical village patients who walked miles to reach us          Many patients arrived in a basket on someone's back

used before we came. I ran the women's department. I did most of the complicated obstetrics and gynaecological operations, as well as treating a multiplicity of illnesses.

Carl did the men patients, and the general and orthopaedic surgery. The overall case load was a grand mixture of almost every illness one could think of. Tropical diseases, infestations

Language class in the garden

with worms of all kinds, hepatitis, dengue fever, Hansen's disease (leprosy) and many other things presented regularly. Later on we were asked to take over a local leprosy settlement where there had been very little care. At that time people with the disease were technically dead as far as the law was concerned, but out in the settlement area we found the most cheerful people one could imagine in the middle of such a hopeless situation. Later we opened a special clinic for them at the hospital led by Dr Pedley from UK, but initially, Carl went to see them regularly and I substituted for him once or twice.

Once when Carl was away, people came from the town to ask me to come to their home to help their 'patient'. This proved to be a goat in obstructed labour, the unborn kid being already dead. For various cultural reasons I was told I had to get the kid out whole, and it proved to be a terrible job. Mary Cundy, a social worker sent out by BMMF, had recently arrived. She comforted the head end of the goat, while I tried to deal with the very small space at the other end through which I was supposed to deliver the dead kid. Finally after much heaving I remembered something I had read in James Heriot's books about Vets in Yorkshire, 'push it up before you try to deliver it', so I did that for a long time and was suddenly able to get it out in one piece. I added the goat onto the hospital ward round for a few days and it did fine, having another kid the next year, but I needed physiotherapy for my aching fingers. The day after the goat success some other people from Tansen brought me a vicious-looking horse with a big skin tumour right beside a strong kicking leg, but as there was no way of protecting any of us from injury while injecting a local anaesthetic, I had to decline.

All of us had to give some time to language study. Nepali is in the Hindi script, with a few variations, grammar is the same as Hindi, but vocabulary, accent and verb endings are quite different.

The hospital became a local school after we left

I got on better than before, thanks to God's intervention in my phonetics and being less concerned about whether I stammered or not since the help in Patna. So altogether we got along fine, with masses of hard work, plenty of wonderful walks, and endless fascinating things to observe and learn about. Unfortunately a few months later I developed hepatitis A (jaundice), probably due to contaminated water on the trail – there were no preventive injections in those days. I got yellower and yellower, lost a huge amount of weight and finally went to Landour in India to convalesce.

When I got back to Tansen I found them laying the foundations of the new hospital. This was to be built on a piece of land about 30 minutes walk away. The locals would not use this land because it was said to be haunted by evil spirits, so we were allowed to take it. We held a prayer service to dedicate the land to God and began building the first temporary rooms for the hospital, plus some very nice brick buildings for staff. At one point Carl said to me, 'Where do you want us to put the ladies' bungalow?' 'Nowhere,' I said. 'Let us have apartments for two people with a nice Nepali style kitchen, a room in which we can entertain, and two bedrooms with small bathrooms attached.' So the old 'ladies' bungalow' idea died there and then, and single people had nice apartment buildings in which they could live independent lives. When part of the old

New house, Tansen – my boss called this 'Marjory praying for the roof'

hospital moved out to the new site, Ingeborg and I moved into one of the apartments, and were *so* thrilled to be away from the severe domestic difficulties of the old house. To have a bathroom instead of having to go out to the garden where there were a few pit latrines was bliss indeed. And the wood-burning *stove* – heaven! We had a compartment to make hot water, a bread oven and a few simple hobs, all designed by our wonderful new missionary Odd Hoftun from Norway. Ingeborg was delighted to have Odd and Tullis, his wife, and their child living near us, and was later to deliver their second child. Odd

was a very skilled engineer and had been involved at a high level in hydro electrics in Norway. Later on he was to be in charge of a very extensive project which created three hydroelectric dams in Nepal. As an added bonus our apartment was only two minutes away from a magnificent view of high Himalayan snow mountains, and we had plenty of opportunity for good evening walks.

There were also plenty of hardships. Food was scarce and much had to be carried up from India. Mail came up by a 'runner' and could be very erratic. In addition, as Christians we often felt oppressed by the blood sacrifices offered to the many idols in the town. But all the difficulties were minimal in comparison with the joy of being there, the beautiful country, the wonderful opportunity to integrate with the people and to serve them physically and spiritually. Once when I was walking down the trail I stopped for the night in one of the inns. Next morning I got up early to wash and brush my teeth just beyond the village, where there was safe water gushing out of a rock near the river. I was all alone, and the birds were beginning to flit around (I was still an avid birdwatcher). The river flowed by, the sun was coming out, the air was balmy. I felt perfectly, totally, happy. I began my morning

In Tansen we were allowed to worship in our own home

prayer thanking God for this wonderful spot where I felt so close to him and so blessed by him. Then I heard the familiar sound of a procession of Nepali carriers rushing down the hill behind me, and knew that the supreme moment was gone and I must return to the job in hand, the walk down the trail towards the busy world.

Politically Nepal was changing. The King continued to create a modified democratic government and so the people had to be taught to vote. Parties were formed, candidates selected, and a trial election was held, the people coming in to vote as if it was a real election. Having learned the skills they finally elected a Government, headed by the King. We did not, of course, get involved in politics, but it was very interesting to watch the procedure in a country new to democracy.

Meanwhile the church was developing. We were allowed to hold worship in our own houses, and the doors were open so people came in. We used both English and the local Nepali language, so everyone got something. Most of the hymns were Nepali tunes and words, some written by patients in bed after surgery. In Nepal the common cultural method of expression was writing songs sung to well-known local tunes, so we were able to build up enough new hymns to make a hymnbook, including also translations of some of the best Western hymns. Worship services were very simple, with no liturgies or rituals other than a simple communion service which we held privately for Christian believers. From the start, the Nepali church developed on its own lines, with help from a few Nepali-speaking people from India who had felt God calling them to come and join the hospital staff. There was never any question of Western leadership of the young church – it was truly indigenous.

The people had great difficulty knowing where to slot us into their caste system. Carl Friedericks was called a Christian Brahmin by some of the Brahmins, this being the highest caste, but otherwise we were a complete enigma. I discovered I was thought to be Carl's first wife whom he had thrown out because I had no children, and he had taken Betty Anne as his second wife. I was making penance for the sin of being childless by working so hard! They also could not understand why the outpatient department was run on a first-come-first-served basis. Usually the Brahmins could take precedence over everything, but we decided to stick to the order of arrival. The thing that really touched the people was that we were all willing to examine their feet if that was what they were complaining of. Feet were generally considered unclean in the spiritual sense, and no one would ever touch an outcaste person's foot. But we did, and if Carl himself held the foot it made a huge impression.

I gradually began to learn how things worked. One day I was asked by a Christian Nepali staff member if he could bring a small group to our house to eat a rice meal. Ingeborg was away, but I gladly gave permission, and found that I also was invited. It was not for some time I discovered what was behind it. There was a man who had become convinced of the truth of the Gospel and really believed that Jesus had died to save him from his sins and to bring him to God. He decided to ask to eat rice with us, that being the visible sign that he was breaking his caste, which he would have to do anyway if he became a Christian. In general the food and other traditions of the Hindu faith were strictly observed. When we travelled, even if we were spending the night at a house owned by one of our grateful patients, because we were technically unclean we had to eat and sleep outside on the verandah.

Despite religious and cultural differences we made friends with the people, for we loved them and they loved us. They could,

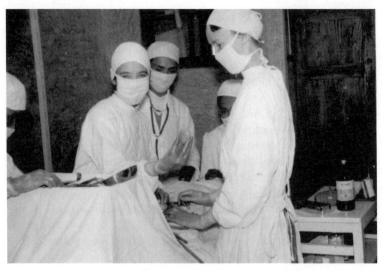

Marjory holding the largest bladder stone in Tansen Hospital to that day, helped by Dr
Pam Dodson who later became director

and did, oppose us on occasions, especially over getting a water
pipe laid for the new hospital, but that never seemed to destroy
the basic love and friendship that existed between us. The fact
that the Friedericks, Elfgaards and Hoftuns all had babies born
in Tansen, made another strong bond. We single people were a
new and different category of women. Once the people realised
we had never been married to the men we worked with, and had
no personal relationship with them, we became an encouragement
to husbandless people in the community. Some of these had been
child widows from early childhood and the people believed these
widows must have sinned in their past lives and so were to blame
for their husband's death.

In the middle of my third year in Nepal I developed a
medical problem that again sent me down to India where I had
first a minor operation and then a major one. I was just on the
point of going back to Nepal when further trouble developed, and
I was hospitalised with a severe infection. I had further surgery
after two months, after which the infection blew up again. So I
ended up going back to the UK (by air for the first time) and did
not get back to Nepal for about nine months. I almost danced back,
turning up my nose at the long trail, greeting my brothel ladies as
I passed their inns, and finally experiencing a wonderful welcome
in Tansen. I was back, and delighted to be there again.

I took up my old tasks with great enthusiasm, and settled down to my final period in Nepal before going on regular furlough. The hospital had developed, although the final building had not yet been started, but we managed very well by using the first row of rooms as outpatients, wards and operating theatre.

A simple nursing training school was opened and I had the privilege of giving some lectures. Two of the students were members of the group that had come over from India to help us. Both of these went on to take proper training when a larger nursing school opened up and did very well. Another member of the class was a widow who had translated from Nepali to Hindi for me in outpatients before I had adequate Nepali. She also worked as a washerwoman and that, combined with her being a widow, made her a despised person in the local community. I tried to teach her to read and signally failed, but this inspired her to spend a bit of her wages on reading lessons from a proper teacher in the town. Some years later she graduated as a nurse and ultimately became Matron in charge of a UMN Hospital in East Nepal, having married a very fine Christian male nurse who had been in my original class.

The medical work remained fascinating, and Carl and I divided up the work on the same lines as before I went off sick. The women's department developed well and continued to provide a fascinating picture of illness in a predominantly untreated population. Later on in my career I recognised that some of our patients were really psychiatric cases. One unhappy young girl periodically stopped talking, and would be brought to the hospital

Tansen Hospital, the first stage to be completed

where we gave her a sedative and, after a good sleep, she woke up talking again. We could do nothing about the cause of the problem which was related to her home situation, but hopefully the love and care we gave her would make her better able to cope.

Throughout this period Nepal was developing. The King died just before I originally went to Tansen, and was replaced by his son, King Mahendru. He was a good man, very keen to see and be seen by his people, so he began riding round Nepal on horseback. The King was believed to be the incarnation of the god Vishnu, and the people believed that if you could catch his eye you would have remission of sins. Consequently he usually wore dark glasses, for it is very tiring to have people constantly trying to stare into your eyes. When he came to Tansen they set up camp on the grassy plain in the centre. Then a big problem arose. The King had to have milk, and for this purpose they tethered a cow near his camp. But due to the noise created by the crowds the cow took fright, broke its tether and was seen no more. One of the King's aides drew his gun and pointed it at the Governor, whose daughter was my patient and quite ill, and demanded a cow at once. So the poor Governor had to ride round the countryside half the night to find a cow, since people did not want to part with such a valuable possession even for the King. The Governor came to see me next morning looking very tired, but at least his daughter was better and he had found a cow. King Mahendru was supposed to open what was ready at the new hospital, consisting only of a few small rooms and the patients' toilets, but enemies turned him back on the way there so he never arrived. We were all dressed in our best, and had prepared a throne for him, so one of the Nepali staff organised something for us. He had written a poem to the King, which he read, and Betty Anne played her violin. We then processed to each room leaving flowers as we went, and when we reached the toilets dropped a flower down every bowl. Finally we went to the future front of the hospital, prayed, sang, dedicated the hospital to God and the people of Tansen, and declared it open.

I continued to love my work and the whole situation, but in May 1960 I had to go on leave. Although I wanted to see my family I shed a few tears as I went down the trail, but slowly cheered up and began to look forward to going home. I also began thinking about what I was going to talk about during my deputation tours in UK, which was an inbuilt part of being a missionary in those days. So I set off down the trail, went on to Bombay (now Mumbai) and sailed for the UK.

# 5

# An unexpected bombshell

I went back to England with three other people from BMMF, and we decided that as we were on an Italian ship stopping at Naples, we could do a little sightseeing across Europe. We went to Naples and Capri where I fulfilled a long ambition of going up to San Michele in Anacapri and then on to Florence. We only had 48 hours there, which was very frustrating, but we did manage an evening open-air concert in the Uffizi Gallery. Then to Rome, which was fabulous, and finally to Milan where I was not allowed into the Cathedral because I was wearing a sleeveless blouse. I told them I was a missionary but it made no difference! 'No' was no. By this time we were experts at small-scale hotels or hostels, and cheap-fare trains, and were really enjoying ourselves. We left Italy by train and stopped off in Switzerland. As we walked into the guest house the receptionist pointed out a tray full of chocolate. With one voice we said 'CHOCOLATE', which we had not seen for five years. The receptionist said, 'Where do you people come from? We had three people here yesterday who said just the same thing when I mentioned chocolate.' So we told her where we had come from, and that we were seriously deprived, so she added an extra bar for good measure. From there we went to the last stop before UK, Paris. My brother and sister had arranged for my mother to meet me there, we had a great reunion and spent five days wandering round. On Sunday she wanted to go to the Scottish Church in Paris and, after a few false starts, we finally found it. The man at the door said 'Come in, you're just in time', and led us to the front seat. No sooner had we sat down than the minister got up, raised his hand and said 'The Peace of God which passeth all understanding guard your hearts', and then proceeded with the benediction, after which the congregation got up to go. Our kind friend at the door was killing himself laughing!

We flew back to the UK where my sister met us. It had been arranged I would have a bedroom in her house and she, her husband and son were very kind to me. Housing missionaries on furlough is never easy for either the missionary or the family, but in those days there was no provision for unmarried women to have a place of their own. Due to often being somewhat isolated, some missionaries can become set in their ways, and retain a lot of ideas that are not really relevant in the church to which they return. By the time I got back to UK a lot of old cultural traditions had changed, and it took me a long time to realise this. For example, styles of clothing had radically changed while I had been overseas, so I had to get used to women in many of the conferences and meetings I spoke at looking like fashion plates, or wearing trousers and relaxing in shorts! I remember the surprise I had when I next went back to India by ship. The first warm day a new missionary appeared on deck in shorts! It was very good for me, and to my credit I said nothing, but just absorbed it as part of the new generation. This all sounds rather ridiculous now, but having been away for ten years, with only one period of leave at the five year mark, it was really difficult to sort out which of my previous social and cultural customs I felt strongly about and which I could ditch in the light of modern church patterns. I was somewhat sensitive about this, based on an experience in Mount Hermon during missionary training. A wonderful person came to give us a talk on her work in some isolated area of the world. Her work was fabulous, and she was totally dedicated to it. But her clothing and appearance were about 50 years out of date and this really detracted from what she was trying to get over. BMMF gave us a clothing allowance on return, so I got advice from my family and spruced myself up in a moderate sort of way and got some decent clothes for my deputation work.

One thing I did at this time was a review of how I had kept myself spiritually alive during the very thrilling time in Nepal and the more difficult first term in India. I had continued steadfastly to read my Bible with a pen in my hand, buying cheap editions in varying English translations, marking them and getting a new one nearly every year. I could not read every day as I was often on call, or operating very early, but always managed to read a few verses and to think about them as I rushed round the hospital. I also took an occasional day off to spend a bit more time reading, praying and thinking. I may have been a bit of a pain in the neck to other people at times, but I was still totally committed to trying to do God's will as I understood it.

At that time I did not understand the dangers of having a lot of 'no-nos', pronounced 'no-nose' – things I thought God did not want me to do, when God's purpose in saving us through Jesus was to give us freedom to live lives full of positive and affirming things, despite the periodic tough patches. Many years later my sister told me that in the early years of my missionary service, when I came home I used to convey an atmosphere of general disapproval, which was the last thing I intended to do! But they forgave me, and later on I had the opportunity to re-examine the whole issue of 'no-nos' and make radical changes.

With regard to church going, I had worshipped mainly in the Urdu speaking church in Lucknow and in Nepal we had our Sunday meetings in a large room, one section of which was curtained off to be our kitchen. As I indicated in the last chapter, the doors were open and people began to drop in. As the number of new songs they wrote increased, it became quite common when we travelled round the trails to hear people in quite small villages belting out their familiar local tunes with the new words attached and I much enjoyed being able to join in.

My major source of keeping going spiritually was learning how to pray 'on the hoof'. I learned that one could really talk with God in one's heart when walking between two wards. He had promised to be with and in us always, so there was absolutely no reason why one could not truly live with him the whole time. Sometimes he was in the background, at others in the foreground, but he was always there. I revelled in this idea of constant belonging, real companionship, and in fact it has never left me even in my darkest times. I know God is there with me, as he had promised when I first gave myself to him. Many years later my sister Vicky told me she began to experience this when she was only eight years old. Things were a bit tough at home and God spoke to her in the dining room. He said 'Vicky, I am going to look after you for the whole of your life', and he did, making her into the doctor so greatly beloved by colleagues, family, patients and friends.

Around this time I learnt something that I have operated on for the rest of my Christian life. I was reading 1 Corinthians chapter 6 and came across verses 19–20. Paul says to the ordinary humble Christian believers: 'Do you not know that your body is a temple of the Holy Spirit, who is in you, whom you have received from

God? You are not our own, you are bought with a price. Therefore honour God with your body'. This made me think, and to look up my various concordances and Greek dictionaries. *Vine's Dictionary of Greek New Testament Words,* for example, made it quite clear that this meant exactly what it said, i.e. that the Holy Spirit lives in our bodies. I still look at this with awe, but also in a very relaxed and practical way. To me it means that every Christian is responsible for carrying God around in the world. It does not mean we will be perfect – we still live on earth as human beings and we shall make mistakes, be difficult and mess things up. But the pathway to forgiveness and renewal of life with our loving God is always open, so we pick ourselves up, ask his forgiveness and strength, and start again.

At this stage of my career this concept became very important to me. Missionaries are traditionally supposed to be evangelists, whatever their professional training. My problem was that I have never been much good at it and I honestly felt that my God-given job was to be the building up of people by caring for their medical and psychological needs, and helping them grow a little in God. But I used to worry about my lack of traditional evangelism gifting! As I came to understand that the Holy Spirit lives within us, I became more confident in accepting that my role as doctor and general helper was exactly what he wanted from me. So I pray for the evangelists and continue to do what God arranges for me.

Meanwhile, the time to start deputation had arrived. This was the second time round and I enjoyed it much more than the first. I had a thrilling story to tell, some unique slides of inland Nepal and felt much more confident of being able to do it. The stammer was still there but was manageable and did not seem to trouble anyone. I was very busy indeed, meeting many people who became life-long friends. To my surprise I also proved to be a very good bookseller, just like my ancestors in the Foyle family.

Time went by and, after a holiday with my mother, I wrote to BMMF asking them to get my Nepal visa for me. By the next mail I got a bombshell. I was not going back to Nepal, but was to take over the hospital in Lucknow, which was in difficulties. I did not know the whole background, but learned that in 1962 a decision had been taken that Kinnaird was of strategic importance and should be modernised and generally upgraded. Otherwise it would 'no longer be considered of importance in the local medical setup', to quote a senior local medical person. It had been decided to make several staffing changes, and I was to be asked to lead it and help establish a modernisation programme. By an administrative oversight no one had consulted me – the office in India thought London had talked with me and London thought India had done it. I felt my heart sink to my boots. I was dumbfounded and very angry. I was heart and soul wrapped up in Nepal, this being strengthened by all my recent deputation work. I loved Tansen and felt it was a part of me, was my home, and Nepal was my adopted country. I revelled in the professional and spiritual work and the life we lived among the mountains. The thought of leaving it was devastating.

The London office asked me to come and see them, which I did, still feeling very angry indeed that I was being so suddenly moved back to a situation I really did not like. Despite the fact that I knew BMMF did not usually operate in this way and that it was obviously an administrative misunderstanding, I felt angry that I had neither been consulted nor given the opportunity to make an informed decision. At one point a senior secretary said, 'I don't think you should go overseas till you get over your anger with God'. 'I am not angry with God,' I retorted, 'I am angry with BMMF.' What was I to do? Should I resign from BMMF and try to get back to Nepal with another Mission group? I could not get over the feeling of desolation at the thought of not being there at a time when the Nepali church and the medical work were developing so rapidly. When UMN heard I was being transferred they also protested and wrote to the office pointing out that if I left Nepal there would be no lady doctor in a large area of Western Nepal.

Looking back I suppose the major reason I felt so devastated was because Nepal had been the place where I felt really fulfilled, and able to make a worthwhile contribution. I had often said to myself, 'Can this be me, doing this job in Nepal, having my own home, living with a lovely Norwegian lady with whom I get on so well, and being loved by and loving the people?' The people had accepted me, stammer and all, and years after I had left I heard that some of the women had come to the Hospital to ask, 'Where is the doctor that speaks like a baby? She really understands us'. I realised God had wonderfully enabled me, given me a job and a location that matched everything I had always hoped for, and I could hardly believe it was all over.

After a few days I became calm enough to think more clearly. I was still committed to being God's servant. What did he want me to do? I cannot now remember what made up my mind for me, but with the greatest reluctance I agreed to go to Lucknow.

As I sailed back to India, I really tried to come to terms with it, but when I became a psychiatrist many years later I looked back and recognised I had begun to experience the classical stages of mourning for the loss of something that had been very important to me. There was little joy on the train journey, just the certainty this was what I had to do, but I did not look forward to it. So once again I was welcomed at Lucknow station, returned to the old Bungalow and communal living, and tried to make the best of it. For a time I worked with the doctor who was leaving, and she picked up how unhappy I was and asked if she could help me. I said, 'Just send me back to Nepal', but of course that was not possible. Before she finally left I spent a week in Nepal with another Mission I thought of joining if I left BMMF, but after a week gazing at the mountains, praying and walking the local trails, I became increasingly aware that this location was not the place for me. So I returned to Lucknow determined to 'gird up the loins of my mind' and work out how I was going to cope with the problems ahead.

When the old senior doctor went to her new location, where she again made a tremendous contribution, I became the senior person in charge and began to think of ways we could save the hospital. We were still treating women and children, and not men, but in that role, unless we could modernise and upgrade, we would become medically redundant due to the opening of several really good women-only units by the local Government. So we began to consider how we could continue to run a good quality women's hospital. I knew nothing at all about hospital administration except that we should form a Board, which we duly did. But no one had any money to give us, and I could not see how we could modernise without a great deal of investment in buildings and equipment. We did get a new autoclave and a few things like that but there was no steady funding to enable us to proceed. Despite much praying by us all, nothing seemed clear. Being me, I flung myself into the problem, although my heart was not really in it, but I did the best I could. We were joined by an excellent BMMF missionary called Noel Matheson, who later married our field leader Alan Norrish after his first wife died. She was a godsend – stable, sensible and very supportive, as were the rest of the staff. One of the first things Noel did was to improve our home and, when she had put up lovely new curtains and a few colourful cushions on the chairs, we all sat round after Church one Sunday in our housecoats with our feet on the coffee tables (very un-Indian I fear), making modified whoopee! She also took over the administrative work, at which she was excellent, and we were able to employ two capable assistants.

As time went by, I began to overwork. I have always handled problems by working hard and this was no exception. I had little background knowledge of the way things worked in Indian hospitals and little idea of what my goal really was. We were trying to create a constitution for the hospital, organise the sparse board meetings, collect ancient statistics, install a battery operated phone system – and I was also busy operating, dealing with difficult obstetric cases, and carrying out full outpatient and inpatient routines. We had two good Indian doctors, but one was elderly and could not be overstretched. That meant more night calls and, although patient numbers were dwindling, the ones we had kept us busy due to staff shortage. The major problem, however, was the underlying grief that refused to go away and the lack of confidence that what I was trying to do would ever come to anything. I did not, of course, recognise this at the time, but later I realised that I had gone back to my old childhood habits of 'trying to be a good girl so that the problems would stop'.

The climax came when I had been there about two years. The BMMF four day annual conference was due to be held in Landour. I was keen that as many people as possible should go, including the Indian doctor, so I was the only doctor left, with a skeleton staff. As soon as they had gone we had an unexpected rush of abnormal midwifery that kept me on the go night and day. I totally stopped sleeping and ate very little. A good Indian friend on the nursing staff was very worried, and very relieved when the conference ended and staff returned. But that made no difference. I was still not sleeping or eating much, and still working as hard as I could to try to deal with it all – the classical signs of clinical depression although I did not recognise them. In God's goodness, a missionary doctor who was being treated for depression at the near-by Nur Manzil Psychiatric Centre asked me to do her routine physical examination. She saw how ill I was and, once I had finished giving her advice, spoke to me plainly about my own health! She advised me to make an appointment with the psychiatrist there, Dr James (Jim) Stringham. He and his social-worker wife Charlotte were building up a centre for treating nationals with mental health problems. It was called Nur Manzil, the House of Light, and had been founded for the Indian people in 1952 by a well known American missionary called Dr E. Stanley

Jones. However, as well as nationals Jim was also starting to get missionaries as patients, for they had high-stress occupations and there had been very little mental health care available to them overseas. Eventually missionaries came from as far afield as Hong Kong, South Africa and all the countries in the Indian sub-continent.

I decided I had better follow my patient's advice, for she had warned me of the serious consequences of not getting help, and Jim gave me an appointment for next day. I went over to see him and was totally unable to return to the hospital. I felt absolutely finished, overcome with fatigue and unresolved grief. They took me into their own home, where I received a long period of wonderful personalised care, helped along by people from my own hospital who came to be with me when I was very ill. My depression eased up slowly with good medication and care, and I became able to start discussing with Jim and Charlotte the various events in my life that had led to this serious illness. One day Jim said something, I don't remember what it was, and I felt as if I had suddenly broken to pieces. I began to cry and, despite fairly heavy medication, I cried for several days. Then one day it began to lift and I realised I was feeling lighter in my mind and heart. A deep well had been opened, I shed the tears I should have shed earlier in my life, and now I could, with God's help, put the pieces together and learn how to live.

I do not intend to do more than write about the major things I experienced, and how I dealt with them, but that will be enough to show that God meant it when he promised all those years ago 'I will never leave you nor forsake you'. There were two major things. The first was the danger of harbouring negative emotions, which I will explain, and the second was that we are told in the Bible to love others *as we love ourselves*. I began to understand that we need to love ourselves as God's new creation, and to respect ourselves as someone he has made and wants to use, however brilliant or slow we are, and however much we have been battered about or handicapped at any stage in our development. I discovered that when we are trying to work out past difficulties in our lives we can be positively rude about ourselves and never give ourselves any credit for the mammoth struggle we may have made to help us cope with the situation. I learned that I needed to respect myself for my childhood struggles to overcome the wounds my home situation had created, the resultant loneliness and the difficulties of having a speech problem in childhood. It sounds crazy, and I assure you I am not, but I begged my own pardon for being rude to myself about my own failings and inadequacies, rather than treating myself with the compassionate understanding I would give a needy patient in the same circumstances. As the days went by I began to be enormously thankful for the way God was moving into my life to bring healing to the damaged areas, and the careful and compassionate way he was bringing me out again to a life of renewed and loving partnership with him for the future.

With regard to harbouring negative emotions like resentment, hatred, bitterness and malice, I had a great deal to learn. I subsequently wrote about this in my book *Honourably Wounded*, for, as I moved towards recovery, I realised how important it was to deal with these 'poisons of the soul'. I asked God to help me learn how to get rid of the load of such emotions in my own life. So first I began to think about anyone I had hurt and, where possible, to ask their forgiveness. I then looked at the unresolved jealousy, resentment, anger and bitterness in my own life. None of this examination was morbid introspection. I was thinking clearly and profitably, and I realised I had a chance to get rid of old, unhealthy emotions, to be forgiven for harbouring them, and to start again with God who loved me and could teach me to live in a more loving and productive way. I brought it all to a conclusion by writing on paper the names of those who needed to forgive me and whom I had not been able to contact. I also wrote a list of all those I wanted to forgive. The Revd and Mrs Eric and Margie Lowe, old friends from BMMF, had written to ask if they could help me, and I asked them to come to Lucknow to give me a private communion. I arranged with Eric that he would give me space during which I could make a clear act of forgiving others and being forgiven myself. The Stringhams joined us, and at the end we all took communion together. I found such a ritual very meaningful indeed and later on in my life I realised what a useful thing it is to give patients with depression something concrete to do.

I think this was a turning point for me, not only in my illness but in my life. Among all the rest of it, I dealt with not being in Nepal and accepted that I had done the right thing in accepting the Lucknow appointment, even though it did not look as if it was going to be concluded in the way we had hoped. When I was sick, Dr Fox, the previous leader, returned from her new appointment to look after the hospital, leaving just before I was well enough to return to work. In her place Dr Mary Eldridge came out from UK for six months. She was, and remains, a very good friend of mine,

Kinnaird Hospital. Mary Eldridge and I toast each other in a local fruit drink

known to us in Lucknow as 'The Relief of Lucknow'. This has a double meaning. In 1857 Indian soldiers mutinied against the British, in modern parlance this now being called the First War of Indian Independence. The famous Sir Henry Havelock who arrived to relieve the British garrison was himself besieged, and in turn was rescued by a strong military force, the whole process being called The Relief of Lucknow, made famous by Lord Tennyson's poem 'Julia's dream'. So Mary modernised history by becoming the latest person to relieve Lucknow! After three months away I slowly returned to work, but three months later my senior doctor became ill from the overwork created by my absence and had to go off sick herself. The financial situation was critical.

To anticipate a later decision, in March 1965 an emergency meeting of the Board was held, at which they all realised that closing the hospital down was the only solution, this later being endorsed by the North India committee and finally agreed to by the Field executive council two months later. By this time I myself had moved on. I was not well enough to carry the huge load of leadership at such a critical time, but since I had not finished my therapy with the Stringhams I needed to remain somewhere near Lucknow until I went on home leave in nine months' time.

We heard there was need of a woman doctor in a village hospital at Kachwa and they would be glad to have me, and agreed to my being away for two days every two weeks to go to

Lucknow. So I packed up and moved to the country, leaving other people to deal with the problems of Kinnaird Hospital's future. An attempt to open men's work failed due to the terms of the original land documents. The Indian Church tried to run it as a tuberculosis unit for a time, but after a month this foundered for much the same reasons as when the Kinnaird was closed. Ultimately the buildings were sold to the Medical College which later opened a child psychiatry unit there. Naturally we felt sad. The Kinnaird had 74 very good years. Was it all wasted, together with the money we had spent on trying to modernise it? I do not think so. I read in my Bible about Mary breaking an alabaster jar of expensive perfume over the Lord's feet. The jar and perfume were costly, but were now broken. It was through the breaking that the Lord was anointed for his forthcoming death on the Cross and burial, which led to our salvation and freedom. So just as there was a creative purpose in what others called waste, so the same thing was true for the breaking of Kinnaird. In reality, for years many wonderful women had poured out their health and strength on the hospital, thousands had been helped, and even today there are still a few people around who boast of having been 'born in Douglas', the local name for Kinnaird. I happened to meet the son of one of them while chatting on a London Underground train recently. Many came to hear of Jesus and his love during those years, and the whole thing was a privileged offering to God, even though I had not personally enjoyed it very much.

One of our patients was from Mecca and brought her son with her

I did, however, enjoy the nine months I spent in Kachwa, my first experience of living in rural India, and I also enjoyed travelling regularly to Lucknow on the train. I became an expert on the movements of trains between Benares and Lucknow, as well as on the railway bird population. The Kachwa staff took care I was not overloaded and I had no administrative responsibility. There were a lot of country walks and I recuperated well. I finished my treatment with the Stringhams and began praying about what to do when it was time to return home. I had a strange feeling that I was learning to live, to enjoy things around me, and to relax in God instead of trying to be a hyper-Christian! I began to trust him to show me what my future was to be when the right time came, and not before, although this important Christian skill took some time to accomplish and is not yet complete!

# 6

# The next adventure

A few months before I was due to go home on leave, I went to an expanded BMMF conference in Landour, which several home council members were attending. I still had no idea what I was going to do next and was waiting eagerly for God to show me. During one of the business sessions a man whose name I did not know got up and expressed the need for a psychiatrist in missions. He felt missionaries had increasingly stressful lives, and it would be a real help if someone who understood their working conditions and spiritual commitments was trained to help them. He then turned to me and said suddenly, 'Would you be interested Marjory? I know your hospital work has just closed down.' Somewhat startled I replied, 'I would be interested, but surely at 43 I am too old to start further postgraduate training?' 'Well', said the Chairman, 'it's a good idea. I know a man called Dr Monty Barker who is a Senior Registrar in psychiatry in a training hospital in Dundee, Scotland. Would you like me to contact him and ask what he thinks?' 'By all means', I said, 'and please let me know as soon as you hear anything'. Afterwards I asked the chairman to be sure to tell Monty that I had been depressed, but was now fine and back at work. Monty Barker was a well known psychiatrist, one of the few people able to remain popular with the evangelical community in a subject viewed with some suspicion. He was academically brilliant, a fine teacher in both psychiatry and the Bible, and respected in both the psychiatric and Christian worlds. He and his wonderful wife Rosemary were to remain my firm friends throughout the rest of my career.

I went back to Kachwa for my last month, during which I got an airmail from Monty to say that he had spoken to Professor Batchelor and they would like me to come to Dundee for an interview two days after I arrived back in UK. The hospital was short of staff and if I was willing to become a junior doctor again, and was found suitable at interview, I would probably get the job.

That all sounded fine on paper, but as soon as I got home I hit a problem and had no time to resolve it before going to Dundee. When I left UK five years previously, we were wearing long wide fully pleated skirts, with heavily padded matching jackets. I had left the outfit in my wardrobe at home, but by the time I returned to UK mini-skirts had arrived, stockings had become tights, and jackets were decidedly skimpy. Unfortunately I had no time to go to the shops before the train left, so I put on the old fashioned outfit and must have looked very odd indeed. Monty met me and later took me to the interview. Professor Bachelor, later Sir Ivor Bachelor, was a small keen-eyed man, somewhat remote in manner, but obviously hugely competent. His interviewing colleague was Dr Aungle, the Medical Director of the Liff Hospital where I would train if successful. They asked me why I was interested in psychiatry and I decided to tell them the whole truth. I explained I had worked in India and Nepal for 16 years or so and been in charge of a hospital. I had become depressed and had to stop work, but was now back at work and very much better. Because I had been ill myself, expatriates and nationals overseas were asking me for mental health care, presuming that after my personal experience I was now an expert! I then said what was apparently music to Prof's ears. I said, 'I am not prepared to try to help people when I know absolutely nothing at all about psychiatry, hence my interest in getting properly qualified'. He positively beamed, and after a few more practical questions asked me to go out of the room. They talked for about ten minutes and then offered me the job for six months 'to see how you like it'. Obviously the truth was 'to see how we like you', but they were too polite to say so. In reality, a middle-aged missionary doctor from India who was wearing an outfit five years out of date, and who had a past history of depression, was not exactly the usual background for a new trainee psychiatrist, so they were taking a risk. I thanked them and said I would like the job, was given a joining date, returned to England and, after a short holiday, collected my scattered belongings and set off for Scotland.

Liff Hospital was just on the edges of Dundee, one of the old style mental hospitals beautifully converted into a more modern setup, plus several modern blocks. The grounds were extensive, and I was housed in a brick-built house, with two bedrooms, a lounge dining room, kitchen and bathroom and lovely grassy slopes outside the window. I discovered I was sharing the house with a very nice young man called Andrew Reid. He was so kind to me. He discovered my Indian background and, realising that I was a bit out of touch with modern Scotland, decided to take me under his wing. We became, and remained, firm friends, as he supported me through my early days and a bit later on I supported him through the nerve-wracking problem of asking a lovely young lady to marry him. Later on I was at their fantastic wedding.

Three junior doctors at Liff: Vi, Claire and I, all dressed up for a party. Note my modern clothes and hair-do!

Professor Batchelor had appointed me to his own unit. Initially Monty Barker took me round and, as he put his hand on the ward door, I said to myself, 'This is *it*, no turning back'. By this time I had bought a few modern clothes so looked a lot better than I felt. Inside I felt like a real 'aged pelican' having been out of medicine in the UK for nearly 20 years. I was an expert in 'real medicine' like tuberculosis, worms of all kinds, typhoid, cholera, smallpox, severely obstructed labour in humans (and goats!) and many other traditional Indian disorders. But I honestly knew nothing at all about mental health. We only had four lectures in my undergraduate training and most of us did not understand a word of them. Very soon after I began working at Liff, I asked Monty, if he could spare time over lunch, to give me a brief run down on mental illnesses. With his typical generosity he taught me and one of my friends once a week for some time, giving us a series of masterly talks on the common mental illnesses. They were superb and helped me understand that mental illness has a structure, and that a diagnosis can be made which forms the basis of good treatment.

My immediate superior was a very beautiful doctor. Rumour had it that she had once been a model – and she certainly looked the part. She taught me how to take a history and examine a patient and I plunged in. I really enjoyed it once I got used to how things worked and soon settled down to a new life. We worked very hard, with a lot of night calls, but I had very good food and a lovely home, containing what to me was a magical novelty, a colour television set. Monty and Rosemary ran a Graduates' Fellowship meeting in their home, so I was able to meet many other Christians who wanted to learn more about their faith, go out on periodic excursions together and support each other during what was quite arduous training.

I learned that I would have to take two exams. In those days the Royal College of Psychiatrists had not been founded, so we all did the Diploma of Psychological Medicine from the university where we were working. Prof. had set up a very good training course, including periodic lectures from celebrities in specialised areas of psychiatry. The first part of my exams was indeed formidable, anatomy and physiology of the nervous system, plus statistics, a working knowledge of neurochemistry, psychology and a few other things I had never heard of. After one very abstruse lecture my beautiful boss Sylvia turned to me and said, 'What did you think of that?' and I said, 'Numb'. But I ploughed on, enjoying the academic and clinical work, entertaining new friends, joining the local church and driving round lovely parts of Scotland in my *new car*, a dream come true. With the help of some of the Polish nurses, who had stayed on in Scotland after refugeeing there to serve in the armed forces during the war, I took up trout fishing. I began to live a full, active and happy life. So often as I went round the wards, wandered up lovely hills, pulled a trout out of the lake, or went to a dinner party I said to myself, 'Can this really be me?' God had put me in green pastures. I had to work very hard – I despaired frequently of getting any information into my India-climate-contaminated brain, but it was all wonderful.

When Andrew Reid got married he moved out and Dr Vi Shannon moved in. She became a life-long friend and later became well-known and respected for her work with adolescents. She was also a member of the Graduates' Fellowship. We got on well, and began entertaining many people in our home, especially foreign students on placement in Dundee University. We have remained friends to this day and, during our infrequent meetings, we often recall the Christmas when we entertained two huge Nigerian women students and could not find chairs big enough for them to sit comfortably!

I found my experience in India helped a lot with some of the work I had to do. For example, I was able to unravel the problems of an African student thought to be suicidal because he

Professor Sir Ivor and Lady Honor Batchelor visit me in Scotland

was wandering round in a confused state with a length of rope in his hand. In reality he had absolutely no suicidal intent and was just using the rope he held to carry out a tribal ritual to clear his mind. I was also able to see some of the increasing numbers of patients who spoke Hindi or Urdu and to get involved in the social problems surrounding their lives. My Indian general medical experience came in handy too. When I was working as the junior doctor in the psychiatric admission ward in the general hospital, I was asked to examine a Liff Hospital patient admitted for removal of a pelvic tumour. When I saw her, I recognised a condition I had often seen in Nepal, asked for a piece of common equipment and promptly relieved her of her non-existent tumour. This was all rather embarrassing for me, as the consultant surgeon, who had not personally examined her, was my good friend. But some of the psychiatric staff at Liff were very pleased that one of their junior house officers had, as they said, 'scored one over the general hospital'. Naturally I made mistakes too. For example, I did not understand the meaning of 'my good brother' in Dundonian English. I went all Freudian and imagined all sorts of psychological conflicts between two family members until the nurses explained it only meant 'my brother-in-law'.

During this period I went on shedding a lot of irrelevant 'no-nos'. They included things like no make-up, no dancing, no theatres or cinemas, long hair and a lot of other trivia. When I was first converted in 1942 these were the norm in some of the Christian Unions and churches, but because I lived mainly overseas I had never experienced the changing culture in the modern UK Christian world. I had therefore continued to operate on an old-fashioned pattern in the social and cultural areas of my life. During my illness I realised how rigid I had become, and that this had sometimes made the people I loved uneasy in my presence. With the Lord's help I began to work out what to do and, when I joined mainstream UK life in Dundee, I thought very carefully about my old 'no-nos'. I realised there was a difference between God's unshakeable commands and social and cultural behaviour patterns. So I never stole, committed adultery, or allowed hatred or bitterness to remain undealt with, these being some of the permanent standards the Bible sets us. But I dropped most of the old no-nos, adding just a few that were relevant to the age and culture patterns in which I lived. This was an important lesson to learn; later on when I was travelling worldwide I was able to make many temporary adjustments to my behaviour during my visit and thus avoid causing unnecessary offence to the people I had come to serve.

I had great fun working out what God wanted me to do with the freedom he gave. I enjoyed going to the hairdresser and getting some trendy clothes, all aimed at fitting in with the culture and generation I was now living in, as well as being suitable for my new status as a psychiatric trainee. I discovered that the social culture of the Graduates' Fellowship included wine at celebration meals and I felt free to join in. This rebounded on my family relationship. I discovered I had been a social embarrassment to them. They always had a glass of wine with their meals and served it at parties. They had to remember to get soft drinks when I was coming and it was all rather awkward. I was glad to accept a little education on wines from my brother and sister-in-law, and to be able to share in the easiest possible way with family celebrations and other social events held in their home. One of these was in my honour, a huge party of all their friends who had ever had India connections! Sometimes the family came to Scotland to see me and we had lovely evenings out at the famous Pitlochry Theatre. I felt I began to reintegrate with my community, without in any way compromising my faith. I tried not to offend other people's principles and, where things were not clearly incompatible with my own faith, would seek to fit in with them. I did not always get it right of course, but that's life!

The dreaded day of our first year exams came but we all passed, so I began to prepare for the second exam, which was predominantly clinical. I enjoyed this work very much – and in 1968 passed the exams and could write DPM after my name. I always felt God had his hand directly on the selection of a patient for me to examine as part of the clinical test. She was a middle-aged lady with poor social circumstances, a lot of environmental stress and recurrent attacks of depression! I had a lot of clinical and personal experience of this type of illness, so it was really no problem to present a fair picture to the examiner and to make a lot of practical suggestions. When I got up to leave the room the examiners said to me, 'Well, you haven't been wasting your time at Liff, have you!' Very encouraging.

I then had to start thinking about what next. I had a few months of my contract to finish before I was free to work elsewhere and had been praying for some time to know God's will. I was offered a permanent job at Liff Hospital, but I was also considering offering to work at Nur Manzil Psychiatric Centre in Lucknow. The Medical Director in Dundee agreed to keep my job offer open for three months while I awaited the outcome of my visa application for Lucknow. This was confirmed in two months, so with expressions of regret on both sides I gave advance notice.

While completing my contract I began to explore the right agency to join when I went back to India. Under the rules of BMMF at that time, anyone staying at home for more than a year had to resign and I had therefore done so when I joined Liff Hospital. So I now needed to seek a new agency. Nur Manzil Psychiatric Centre in Lucknow had been linked for many years with the United Methodist Church in USA but was now fully under the control of the Indian Methodist Church. They did not have enough money to pay for me to join them and I was uncertain about my funding. I then heard that one of the officials from the Missions department of the United Methodist Church of America was passing through Edinburgh, so I went over to see him. After discussion he offered me a monthly salary plus return fares to India and back, to be paid by the Board in USA. There would also be pension rights if I did more than a certain number of years. I decided to accept this, and was also able to forge a new link with BMMF, now called Interserve. I became a Field Partner. This meant they did not have jurisdiction over my movements, but would care for me personally in a pastoral capacity, for which I was to be very grateful as the years went by.

Two weeks before I was due to leave Dundee I developed severe flu which kept me in bed till the end of my contract with Liff. During that time I discovered that if I added £5 to the air fare that I was allowed, I could go to India by sea, sailing round the Cape to get there because the Suez Canal was closed. The voyage would therefore take six weeks rather than 16 days. That seemed like a great idea to me, and was exactly what I did. After a weepy farewell on Dundee station and a quick visit to London to gather all my stuff and send it off by sea, I got on the train across Europe and picked up the ship in Venice. We had six weeks of bliss. We steamed round the Mediterranean and enjoyed Christmas at sea, when the junior crew asked a few of us to see their Christmas tree in their quarters and sing carols with them. At Cape Town we were joined by a group of mixed-colour South African school teachers travelling from the Cape to Pakistan and back for their Christmas holidays. They looked a bit uncertain when they arrived, as was common in the apartheid era, but an accidental encounter sorted it out. I had been changing into my swimming costume in the pool side cloakroom when a black South African girl came in. She said 'Excuse me' and began to go out, obviously intending to wait till the 'white person' had finished. Realising what was happening I rushed out, grabbed her hand, said 'Come in and change', and then we went out together hand in hand and plunged into the pool. From that moment the atmosphere changed, the teachers relaxed, and we became 'Economy Class United', all of us having fun.

So we sailed across the Indian Ocean, until we arrived at Bombay, little changed from my first experience in 1949. There was no one to meet me at the docks so I got a taxi and went to the Bombay office. No one was there either, so I sat on the doorstep till they turned up, watching the old familiar India go by. The gentleman in charge was most apologetic, but he had not been informed that I was coming. All ended well and after completing a few bits of business I got back onto the familiar train and went to Lucknow.

# 7

# All change again

Before I accepted the appointment as psychiatrist in Nur Manzil Psychiatric Centre, I had laid down the condition that under no circumstances would I ever be Director. Dr Stringham was due to retire in 1970, his successor was a brilliant young Indian psychiatrist called Dr Chander and all I wanted was to work as a psychiatrist under his leadership. The staff at Nur Manzil lived just outside the inner hospital wall and I was given a rather hot flat up a back stairway looking out over the side street. The great advantage was that I could go further up these stairs and sleep on the roof in the hot weather, protected by the Business Manager's three sons who also slept on the roof. The disadvantage was that the verandah joining my sitting room and bedroom was protected only by wire screening and not by glass or wooden shutters, so I was totally exposed to the hot afternoon winds, renowned as a killer. Some time later Bishop Lance, chairman of our Board as well as area Bishop, found out how hot it was and asked why I did not put in air conditioning. I explained I could not afford it, which rather shocked him and after enquiring about my salary he discovered I was being paid only two thirds of what I was supposed to get. He immediately wrote to the USA office and got the mistake rectified, so I was able to install a 'desert cooler', the old established way of air cooling in India, which was much cheaper than air conditioning. With my enhanced salary I was able to save money for the first time ever, so diverted one-third of my salary to my bank in the UK, much to the relief of my long suffering bank manager.

I enjoyed being back. I had obviously considered the dangers of returning to work in the hospital where I had received my own treatment and the wisdom of returning to Lucknow at all. I was, however, 100% sure this was what God wanted, as shown by the rapidity with which I obtained the hard-to-get visa for India. I felt sure I was right to go back to Lucknow, despite my real regrets at leaving Scotland. In the event I had absolutely no trouble settling in and decided to change to Indian dress permanently as more suitable for both me and the hospital. I also had to revise my rusty language skills to fit the new situation but it all came back fairly quickly. I was glad to have my own home, freedom to do what I wanted in my spare time and the opportunity to make new friends as well as finding some of the old ones. I joined the English-speaking church next door, became a choir member in two churches, and enjoyed the rehearsals and our major concerts at Christmas and Easter. The hospital was surrounded by a lovely garden, plus the garden inside the hospital, so I kept up my birdwatching skills daily as I trotted around on my duties.

I loved the work. Most of our patients were Indian, but we still had some missionaries coming to see Dr Stringham. The flood of expatriates had come to an end, missionary patients either getting better or going home, and there were fewer new missionaries because of visa and other restrictions. Our Indian Christian and non-Christian patients came from both local and outlying areas, so we had to try to choose a multilingual staff. I was really happy and was glad to have only clinical responsibilities, leaving all the administration to other people.

When Dr and Mrs Stringham retired we had a lot of tear-filled leaving parties and then we settled down to life under Dr Chander. This was good, but sadly was not to last long. The Christian Medical College Ludhiana, one of the most prestigious colleges in North India, intended to strengthen its psychiatric department and contacted Dr Chander to ask if he would take over leadership. His wife was an anaesthetist and they also offered her a job, so in the end they decided to go. The Board of Directors met to decide what they would do about Nur Manzil leadership and in the end agreed to ask me to take it on. I am not just being modest when I say I know they would not have chosen me had there been anyone else. Part of the problem was that I was British not American and even though the ex-American Methodist work in India was now nationalised, they were accustomed to having contact with the US through the Stringhams. I was a member of a church in the UK and also of the Indian Methodist church in India, but that was a very different setup from having an American or an Indian in charge.

Despite the difficulties I foresaw, and after much prayer, I decided I would do what God was indicating, rather than letting

The unending paperwork that landed on my desk at Nur Manzil

Nur Manzil founder from lack of leadership. In a way I was back in the old Lucknow situation, but there was a much better administrative foundation to the hospital. The Bishop, whom I knew and liked, was Chairman of the Board and there was a good Executive Committee. I presumed the finances would not be such a struggle as in the Zenana Hospital, although events were to prove me wrong. Anyway, I decided it was right for me to accept the job. The very first morning of my 'reign', one of the servants who had a long standing grudge against someone on the hospital staff began letting off at me before the waiting outpatients. However, a Hospital Administrator had recently been appointed, so I left it to him to sort out.

The implications of my appointment became clear to me a few days later when I studied the Hospital Constitution. As Clinical Director I was responsible not only for the medical care, but also acted as secretary to the Board of Governors and various committees, with responsibility for preparing reports, agendas for meetings, circulation of minutes and many other minutiae. My immediate task therefore was to master all the recent committee documents and then to get my finger on the hospital pulse.

One good thing was that I had a lovely new apartment to go with the job. It was on the ground floor, with a large sitting room, a garden right outside the window, two bedrooms, a dining room, a kitchen, and a room I could use as my study. It was considerably cooler than the old one and I boosted this very easily with my faithful desert cooler. Another good thing was getting to know Bishop Lance and his wife. He was a remarkable man, brimming with good ideas and was always most helpful to me. I got into the habit of going to see him every six months where I would tell him my troubles and he would tell me some of his, his wife comforting us by providing tea and cakes. They loved joining the Christmas parties I gave when my family began to visit me, and it was good to have such great support when Board meetings became a bit difficult.

Dr John Mathai, one of my junior staff, became a consultant in child psychiatry in Australia

My next job was to review the hospital work. I looked closely at the overall programme at Nur Manzil and retained the best parts of it. The major thing to be preserved was the individual care of each patient. Their treatment was the same in some aspects, but each one had different problems and individualisation was an essential which I sought to protect. I continued the daily meeting to discuss new cases, and the Saturday morning lecture to patients followed by a dedicated hour for commercial drug travellers to meet us, closing the week with a combined staff meeting to discuss patient care. I made changes to various in-patient and treatment routines, all of which seemed to work out well. One thing I realised was that it would take too much time for me to keep an eye on staff welfare by allotting individual time for that purpose alone, so I decided to combine it with the private meeting I had with them every two weeks for discussion of their patient work. It was not a marvellous arrangement but I knew they were very supportive of each other and would only need to talk to me about something very major.

Over the years I was joined by a series of junior doctors, some being 'scholarship bond' doctors from various Indian Christian Medical Colleges. These had received a scholarship to study and

Dr Narayan and family went from Nur Manzil, India, to Liff Hospital, Dundee, for further studies. My sister-in-law went to see them. He became a consultant in child psychiatry in the UK

after graduating were asked to give three years to working in Methodist Hospitals. I had some very good young doctors through this scheme, all of whom went on to fine careers. Several Hindu and Christian psychiatrists joined the staff for varying periods of time and were a great help to us. Through an arrangement with Liff Hospital, four of my staff went to the UK for further studies, two of them already having psychiatric qualifications from India. Dr Emmanuel, another scholarship bond doctor, left to get his higher psychiatric qualifications in Lucknow Medical College and, a few years after I had retired, became the very successful Director of Nur Manzil. An unusual applicant to work at Nur Manzil was Dr Thomas Gnanamuthu. He was an older man who had worked for years as a surgeon in a Methodist Hospital in South India. He wrote and asked me if he could come for six months, explaining that he felt God's calling to give up surgery and open a counselling unit in Bangalore. Realising he would need knowledge of mental illness he felt Nur Manzil was the best place to get it. Being a choirmaster and musician as well as a doctor, he was a great asset to both hospital and church. At the end of six months he realised he needed to know more, so he applied to return on a longer term basis together with his wife and youngest child, who was a piano teacher. They joined us and Thomas continued his training, becoming a very wise and reliable colleague. Many of these doctors have remained my personal friends. The nursing staff was led by a series of very capable senior nurses, some of whom had received their basic training at Kinnaird. The team was completed by an occupational therapist, a clinical psychologist and a social worker. There were fine workers in the administrative and domestic areas. Perhaps the strength of the hospital inpatient department was related to a group of ward attendants who had been trained to do various tasks inside the hospital, and they were an enormous help in the daily routine.

I was always very keen on teaching and tried to give as much clinically oriented teaching as possible during ward rounds, case conferences and periodic lectures. The snag was, as I realised later, that I was not really providing enough advanced training for the newly qualified psychiatrists and the nursing staff. It would have been better to have handed this part of the programme over to one of them, but somehow I never got round to organising it, which I regret. As outreach, I enjoyed doing a course of lectures for the YMCA in New Delhi and periodically lectured to the local Jail Training School for prison officers. I had the interesting experience of lecturing to a group of monks at their annual conference and to the staff of the nearby Isabella Thoburn College, another ex-American Methodist Foundation.

One great experience was sharing a platform with Mother Theresa at the opening of a home for leprosy patients. I was a stop-gap, the person invited having to pull out unexpectedly. I was asked to speak on 'The mental health problems of leprosy patients' and was able to draw on my experience in the Leprosy Colony in Nepal. Afterwards Mother Theresa came up to me, gave me a big hug and said, 'You and I together, doctor, can do great things for God'. I felt it was a real benediction.

The Hospital itself was an old Mughal building with a history of being very active in the Indian Mutiny or, speaking as an Indian, the First War of Indian Independence, in 1857. In the evenings the owner, an Indian queen, used to ride out of Nur Manzil on an elephant to go and see how the besieged British in the nearby Residency were getting on. After the war was over the building was bought by an Indian gentleman of Portuguese ancestry, later it became the YMCA and was finally bought for the Psychiatric Centre. Our main buildings were still the original

| The new Nur Manzil building | Dr Emmanuel, Director of Nur Manzil, and a member of the ward staff |

Mughal construction, very beautiful, with a wonderful dome on top, but unfortunately the Mughals knew nothing about damp coursing so it was damp. We were all sad when years after I had gone it became unsafe and had to be pulled down, although it was replaced by a fine modern building. The residential part of the hospital was purpose-built round a large circle with good grass lawns in the centre. The gardeners got fed up of preparing flower beds when a small series of patients decided to eat the flowers, but we persevered. For patient protection the circle doors were kept locked, not so much to keep the patients in as to keep undesirable people out! There was an occupational therapy department, a television room, two ward areas with several beds and a large collection of double rooms. On one side of the circle was the chapel where we held morning prayers six days a week and a special prayer service every Tuesday evening. Patients were free to come to any of these, whatever their religion.

We had a wonderful mixture of patients. A trickle of people from the missionary community still came, but since most areas now had some sort of local mental health care available, we were not so urgently needed. We were recognised as a treatment centre for workers in the Government offices of a North Eastern state in

India and by the leader of a small Muslim group based in Bombay, but most patients came because they had heard about us from other patients. At that time we were able to allocate two hours for each new patient interview, which included discussion with the relatives, so it was very satisfying. One patient owned a mango orchard in the hills, so we always made sure her annual follow-up appointment was booked for the mango season! Inevitably there was a lot of family-oriented work because, particularly in that community, much of the care needed was related to the family and wider caste or faith group structures.

Clinically, the work was much as it would be in other countries, all the usual mental health problems presenting in various forms. However, the different cultural backgrounds and languages led to patients using different expressions to describe their symptoms. I was glad to come across a paper written in Pakistan which found that when patients complained of pain at the top of the head they were usually suffering from depression. While we gave Western-style treatment, we put a strong emphasis on family involvement, including care for family members as well as the patient, and we found that living in a mixed cultural and religious group was often very helpful to the inpatients. I tried to set up a group therapy programme carried out by the national doctors, but I made the mistake of introducing a Western pattern, which the other doctors recognised at once as unworkable. Later on they told me they never did what I said in this area, and were surprised when I said, 'Thank goodness, because I was totally wrong!'

To boost patient recovery I instituted a monthly tea party cum patient programme to which patients' relatives could come. This was a most moving event. Because the patients lived in a community and helped each other, it was wonderful to see someone who was initially very sick indeed be encouraged by the other patients to get all dressed up and recite a few verses at the tea party. I used to sit and cry!

All in all the clinical work was very satisfying, but other aspects were in dire trouble. Very shortly after I took over I was informed that two major grants from New York, which had apparently been decreasing annually since before I took over, would now be totally withdrawn. These had provided a significant part of our funding. I reported this to the Executive Committee and, to this day, have no recollection of what we decided to do. Probably we just decided to work hard, try to make richer people pay a bit more while we continued to help the poor – and pray to

God to help us! I was asked by the Board to speak at a meeting of the regional Methodist Church leaders to outline our situation, but they clearly did not believe me. (This was one of the difficulties of being from the West; one was automatically supposed to be rich, and it would have been much better if one of the Indian staff had done it.) Despite this we survived and were still in business each time I had to give the annual report.

Certain personal things were happening too. During my term of office as Nur Manzil Director, the Royal College of Psychiatrists was founded in London. For those unfamiliar with British qualifications, undergraduate degrees in medical subjects are awarded by University examinations, MBBS, MBChB, BM, or MB BCh being the initials of the degrees awarded. These make us doctors and are the equivalent of the MD degree in USA. Degrees for higher specialist qualifications are provided by the Royal Colleges, so there are, for example, separate Royal Colleges for Physicians, Surgeons, Anaesthetists, General Practitioners, etc. The psychiatrists had for a long time been a part of the Physicians College and it was felt they should become independent. A Royal charter to found its own College was granted and so the Royal College of Psychiatrists was born in 1971, creating its own new postgraduate degree, the MRCPsych. The authorities wrote to anyone who held a Diploma in Psychological Medicine and was working in a senior position, and invited us to apply for exemption from the examination for the award of the new qualification. I duly did this, but because I was working overseas was asked to come to London for a twenty minute oral examination. I got permission for special leave and, in 1973, after an interesting interview, came away with the MRCPsych to add to my name. This was important for my future work as well as for Nur Manzil's reputation, so I was delighted. In 1980, after recommendation by Prof. Batchelor and others, I was honoured by being elected a Fellow of the College and became FRCPsych, again very good for Nur Manzil.

After my Membership interview in London I spent three weeks in my lovely Scottish hideout. Before taking up my appointment at Nur Manzil I had negotiated a two-year and nine months period of service overseas with three months in UK. I was not going to work for five years at a stretch as I had done before. Just before I was due for the first break, a colleague I had worked with in Dundee wrote to me asking if I would like the loan of a free apartment in a country estate in Scotland. WOULD I LIKE IT? I said 'Yes please' immediately, and each time I came home,

Back to my Scottish paradise for a rest

after spending ten days with my family in England I went up to Scotland for eight weeks. It was paradise indeed. There was a nice apartment in the old house, access to a huge lake ('loch' in Scotland) with some rebellious trout in it, hills to walk in, a wonderful theatre nearby, a car that gave me total freedom to explore remoter areas of Scotland and, best of all, my family and friends were able to come up and stay with me.

The estate was north of a lovely small town called Pitlochry and the owners were very kind to me. It was wonderfully relaxing. Sometimes I would go up to the loch about 9 am with a flask of tea, a fishing rod, and some food, and get so lost in it all that it was often 6 pm before I became aware that the day had gone. I owe the owner, his mother and the rest of the family a great debt. I keep a photo of my favourite spot by the loch on my desk and sometimes sit gazing at it and almost smelling the sweet air. On arrival I usually spent ten days alone with absolutely no set programme, and would then start entertaining my family and friends. I worshipped at the small Scottish church, but did *no* deputation work. I could not have designed it better, and I was privileged to go there several times during my appointment to Nur Manzil. I am sure these breaks were the reason I was able to carry the heavy work load in India. Ever since then, if I have been in a tight corner or a difficult place I rest my mind by imagining I am beside the loch, watching a trout rise in the rippled water. Very

The famous loch. Only suicidal fish get caught

relaxing in the middle of a busy and fractious committee meeting! On one of my visits there I saw something that is a permanent part of my memory bank. We had heavy rain for three days and nights. About 9 pm on the third evening the clouds began to lift, and everything turned bright gold. I grabbed a rod and rushed up to the loch. When I got there I could not fish, I just sat on the bank and watched a marvellous sight. Because trout feed near the surface of water, they had been starved for three days. They all came to the surface at once, grabbing whatever food they could find and the golden declining sun turned them into a mass of snapping golden fish. There were so many that the surface of the water looked as if it was boiling. I sat there for more than an hour, hardly daring to breathe in case I scared the fish away.

To return to India, in 1975 we were due to celebrate the Silver Jubilee of Nur Manzil's foundation, and I suggested to the Board that we try to raise funds to rebuild the men's ward. This was a part of the old YMCA and was in a shocking state. I visualised keeping the six-bed ward and sprucing it up and, in place of the crumbling old wards, creating new two-bed units with kitchen and bathroom. We had no money of course, but we all had plenty of experience of praying to God for money and I felt sure if we went ahead with the planning we would get the funds. The Board agreed it was worth giving it a try and fairly soon after that I met some Dutch friends. They told me of the ECCO, a project in Holland that combined with

I returned to Nur Manzil in 2000 for the Golden Jubilee

Government to fund special projects in the Third World. I wrote to them, they came to see the hospital and gave us the money. It was just fantastic. Although there were plenty of problems, it all flowed on from there and on 1 September 1979 we celebrated the opening of the new men's wing. Next morning I popped in to see the new occupants and they raised a cup of tea to me and said 'We are all happy now'. Actually the floor surface was not right and never improved despite being re-done, but otherwise everything looked just lovely.

Another thing that kept me going during these busy years was frequent visits from my family. Sadly my mother had died while I was overseas but she would not have been able to visit me anyway. Family visits began in 1972 when my dearly loved sister-in-law asked if she could come over for her three months sabbatical leave from the BBC. They had given her a research project and I was able to send her safely all over India by arranging for missionary families to look after her. The next year she persuaded my brother to come and that started a regular pattern of Christmas visits. We would spend two weeks away on holiday and then we all went back to Lucknow for Christmas. One year my sister came and we followed the same pattern. The hospital staff and patients loved my family, and there were real tears every year when they went back to England.

During my last three years at Nur Manzil things became somewhat difficult. For a reason I never knew, a small group of men serving on a committee I had to attend ganged up against the hospital, targeting me as the Director. They would stand up and shout at me, and made things as difficult as they could. By that time I was very tired and it usually reduced me to tears. However, just once I had an opportunity to add a little humour to the situation – and so be in command rather than a victim. I had to give a report on Nur Manzil to a conference, so I wrote it and began to present it in English, which was the lingua franca of the meetings. One of these men got up and said, 'We do not understand English, give your report in Hindi'. I immediately translated it into reasonable Hindi. Then another got up and said, 'We don't speak Hindi, we speak Urdu', and again I was enabled to give the same report in Urdu. Then I said sweetly, 'Are there any Nepali speakers here? If so I can give it in Nepali', at which everyone laughed, the atmosphere lightened, and we got on with the business. During this period there were also financial and staff-related problems, although we were still financially viable, and finally my health began to break down with repeated attacks of Asian flu. So I did some hard thinking and praying and decided I would put in a three-year resignation notice of leaving in May 1981, six months before my 60th birthday. I had UK-leave due before then which would enable me to carry on till I retired.

Although I would be retiring when nearly 60 I did not feel my work was at an end, so once more I began to pray that God would guide me. I continued to pray, because I never got rid of the feeling that he had a new job for me related to missionary mental health. I was able to discuss this vague idea with the local BMMF leader, Hester Dain (then Hester Quirk), and she began to correspond with the BMMF London office about the possibility of my visiting every country where BMMF had personnel in order to counsel missionaries and lead seminars on mental health and stress-related topics. In July 1978 I wrote in my prayer letter, 'I am currently working on a tentative plan that would enable me to work peripatetically for 1982/83. I would like to visit six Asian countries during the two years, staying in each place for three months, with a break in England half way through. During my stay I plan to see missionaries and other patients on request, conduct a counselling course for any senior people that wanted to come, and try to teach simple psychiatry to rural Mission Hospital staff. I have already had requests for such a service but have had to postpone any thought of it for the time being. I would like to make it a joint mission project but this may not work out.' This topic turned up in every prayer letter for the next two years, and in 1980 I wrote, 'My plans for the future are still up in the air. I feel I have a further contribution to make, particularly to missionaries and national church workers. I am still hoping to spend time in four countries after retiring from Nur Manzil. I am, however, open to the Lord's leading on this and would value your prayers. It is not possible to make any plans, everything is too vague, but I am content to plan as wisely as I can and leave the rest to God to work out.' From then on I remained in correspondence with the BMMF London and Indian offices about ways and means by which this could be accomplished. We also discussed a tentative outline of my possible renewed membership of BMMF, but I admit I was still not 100% sure this was what God wanted.

Time went by and God began to guide very clearly. Two BMMF psychiatrists, both Australians, married, with children, offered their services. One would come when I left in 1981 and the other some time later after language study. This was magnificent. But I needed God to clarify my thinking so that I was 100% sure the travelling programme I had been thinking of, and in which others were showing interest, would be the right thing to do. It seemed crazy really, for I was quite elderly, had no experience of mobile ministry and, anyway, had I the skills and knowledge to accomplish it?

With these questions in mind I attended the annual BMMF conference in Delhi. During the last evening meeting I had a very real experience with God. At that time Nur Manzil's problem was solved but mine was not. My future was still a collection of 'ifs and buts', and I needed to know clearly what God's will was. I had read of people 'storming the gates of heaven' without really understanding what it meant, but as we got near the end of the last meeting I was seized with a spirit of very deep prayer in which I felt free to speak to God again about my dilemma and to tell him I needed to know his will *now*. I was leaving India in a few weeks, and if he really did want me to start travelling in Asia I had various passport formalities to complete if I intended to come back. I simply said, with reverence but total freedom, 'Lord I need you to tell me now', and he did. He put a blueprint into my mind of what I was to do. My old thoughts about returning to Asia for two years were just right and I was to go first to Bangladesh, then India, Pakistan and Nepal. I was to do just what had been in my mind for two years, see missionaries who wanted to discuss problems, give them supportive lectures and talks, give lectures in simple psychiatry to the staff members of Christian rural mission hospitals and make myself useful in any other way that came up. At last it was crystal clear in my mind. Being me, my first reaction was tears!

After the meeting was finished, I dashed up onto the platform where a great friend of mine had been playing his guitar

Goodbye to Nur Manzil 1980. My successor, Dr Hickingbotham

and leading the closing worship. I flung myself into his arms and said, 'God has guided me and I really don't know how it will all happen, but I know this is what he wants'. He and his wife talked with me, then we all prayed and I went off knowing clearly what was ahead of me, and feeling very relieved. I was now able to deal with all the business involved in leaving India, could begin to think of my programme more realistically, and to make plans for the best use of my time back in UK. My last prayer letter from India in April 1981 said, 'Please pray for me in this unstructured venture. I have felt a constraint to do this for some time and shall need your prayer support as I set off', which has remained my constant request ever since.

In my last few weeks in India, the 'retirement process' occupied much of my time. Dr and Mrs Hickingbotham arrived, the first of our new Australian psychiatrists, and were formally installed in my place. Then it was time for the farewell ceremonies to begin. They lasted several days, so they must have been glad to see me go! First we had a wonderful church service during which the pastor said he wanted to talk about my future in baseball terms. I do not understand baseball but gleaned from what he said that God was preparing me to set off again on a new kind of service. Finally, he and the Bishop laid hands on my head and prayed for me to know and to do God's will. We then had the customary tea party with speeches and garlands, followed after a few days by a big Indian/Muslim style concert. The main feature was a cultural song called a 'kawali', which was a Lucknow speciality. They sang about my career, and included many jokes in classical Urdu, some of which I understood. There were speeches and more songs, followed by a lovely meal together. I also gave parties for all the staff and for my local friends and colleagues, so it was a busy eating time as well as everything else. I packed things up and sent the boxes back to the UK where the head of BMMF kindly put them in his garage till I finally returned to open them six years later. Then the last day arrived and I was actually going, my 32 years in conventional medical mission work had come to an end.

Goodbye to Nur Manzil 1980.
The Bishop and pastor of the church
pray for my future

I was given traditional Indian garlands up to my eyebrows, and cried all the way to the airport. This rather unusual spectacle of a Westerner in floods of tears made the airport security staff rather suspicious, so they insisted I took off all the garlands and searched me very thoroughly, but finally I arrived in the departure lounge to go to Delhi and then to the UK.

During the next few weeks I received letters from various mission authorities asking me to visit the four countries God had spoken to me about, giving dates for my visits and making things very clear. It was immediately obvious that my work would not be confined to BMMF personnel, for the requests that I should visit their locations came from mission leaders of several different nationalities and groups. I talked again with BMMF and became first a Field Partner and then a little later had a period of full membership. They agreed to my suggestion that the actual arrangement of the programme be left to me, so that I could be flexible and make changes where it proved necessary. It was significant that a large donation was received from the Panahpur Trust, whose ongoing financial support would later on enable me to continue a much wider ministry than we originally envisaged. My debt to them is incalculable.

One major problem, which also kept popping up in my prayer letters, was housing. I had nowhere to call my own home and my brother and sister-in-law very kindly asked me to stay with them when I was in UK. They were wonderful to me during the four years their home was my base and I am deeply grateful to them for putting up with my comings and goings, but I was sure God had a plan for my housing. Because the right time had not yet come, the solution had to wait for some years, and in chapter 10, I will describe how God kept his promise that he would supply all my needs.

Meanwhile, it was still 1981, and after a brief stay in London I went to Scotland, very pleased indeed to return to the flat on the lovely Perthshire estate. My family came to visit me in turns. In preparation for my travelling role I wanted to spend a few months reading, and was able to rent a room and then a flat in the Cornish village from which my grandfather came and where my mother was born. The weather was foul, raining a lot of the time, but I managed to walk and swim as well as reading and thinking. For the last two weeks my family joined me, and then I returned to London fit and prepared for what lay ahead.

# 8

# A biblical suitcase

As I contemplated my future I realised I would need a new and very special suitcase. It would have to contain enough clothes for at least a year, lecture notes, the one large textbook I allowed myself, plus all the other oddments such as hair dryers that women require when travelling. It would have to be strong and on wheels (built-in trolleys had not yet arrived) and adequately waterproof.

The start of my mobile work in 1981, Bangladesh.
Note typewriter, no computers!

So I went to a big store in London, explained what I was going to do and we looked around. I settled on one that looked very strong but they said it would probably only last me a year with the hard wear I was going to give it. Twenty-five years later it was still in very good condition and by that time I had named it my 'biblical suitcase', because I felt like the children of Israel whose shoes and clothes never wore out as they wandered round and round the desert! But trolley cases had now arrived so I bought one and gave my biblical one to an Oxfam charity shop. I hope someone else is now enjoying owning it.

On 2 January 1982 I set off for Asia, and travelled a full 15 months before returning to the UK. During this period I had no settled home, but usually the hosts who had invited me to visit their country arranged for a room for me which became my permanent base until I moved on to the next country. My basic principle was that I would go to see personnel where they worked, unless of course I had just been invited for a central conference. In this way I felt I would get a clearer idea of the local stress factors, even though it meant a lot of travelling for me. I never regretted this policy. After a few days in India I went on to Bangladesh, my first visit there. The country had only fairly recently become independent from Pakistan, changing its name from East Pakistan to 'Bangla Desh', the land of the Bengalis. It was difficult to know how to dress or behave because the newly independent culture was not really established, but things were buzzing with enthusiasm, much the same as India had been just after Independence – and I found it very stimulating.

I do not intend to give all the details of my visits to 40 different countries, some of them more than once. This would be tedious to read, but I will try to pick out things of special importance and interest in some of the places I visited. Basically, my work included six different aspects:

- Teaching staff in rural Christian hospitals and small clinics something about mental illness, including causation, diagnosis and treatment. This also included examining patients selected by the hospital for me to see.
- Meeting with individual missionaries on request to hear their problems and give advice about what to do. This also included discussing children's needs.
- Meeting with mission leaders in home and overseas countries.
- Giving lectures, conference talks and occasionally preaching a sermon, as requested by nationals and missionaries.
- Meeting local psychiatrists working in government psychiatric units.

- Meeting and working with those involved in setting up a worldwide organisation for overall care of missionaries, now called *Membercare*.

The latter work developed after I had been travelling for some years, largely because the World Evangelical Alliance asked two excellent psychologists to start travelling and investigate what was going on worldwide. To antedate what developed later, a world movement called *Membercare* was established, which is still being developed. People from many of the countries sending missionaries overseas, or to work in other parts of their own countries, required information about the best way to care for their personnel. Through our own increasing understanding of missionary stressors, and other basic problems, we were able to pass this information on and work together to establish better and more healthy conditions for people doing what was often very high stress work. The care was of course broad-based, including good selection and training before going overseas, good administration, the availability of mental and physical health care in the working location, assistance in problem solving such as deciding where and how to educate the children, and in-service personnel care, such as dealing with their major stressors in the most productive way. As I travelled round I kept very careful notes, and collected as much material as I could so that we would be able to present an accurate picture during *Membercare* discussions and the conferences that developed later on. My American friends, Kelly and Dave, became the leaders in this new movement, and I was very glad to be present at some of the early gatherings where we felt very certain of the presence and power of the Lord as we planned to assist his servants worldwide.

Bangladesh was an excellent place to start my new ministry. I was cared for by a lovely family and given a large bedroom with space to see patients. Incidentally, my use of the word 'patients' is a habit – what I mean is anyone who wanted to talk privately with me. An extensive tour had been organised and an outline of the programme was given me. I immediately began to prepare my lectures for the rural hospital staff, some of which would be given by interpretation. I had done a lot of this type of simple teaching in India, so was able to transfer it to a clear outline of the mental health problems with which the staff might have to deal. Because PowerPoint® had not yet been invented, and electricity was not always available anyway, I put it all on big flipcharts, sometimes having vernacular ones prepared as well. The flipcharts proved more rugged than I was, appearing never to show signs of wear and tear – and by the end were translated into several languages.

I stayed in Bangladesh for eight weeks, during which I visited eleven different locations. As an example of the total case load, I gave 28 lectures, saw 29 complex patients and many shorter cases. I also made three professional visits to local psychiatric units. I found it all most interesting and discovered I was really happy with this type of work because it was so stimulating. Travel was often tough and living conditions were not always easy, but it was endlessly fascinating. During a visit to a national Government Hospital mental health unit I found that the head doctor had worked at my old Dundee Hospital, leaving just before I came, so we were delighted to meet each other. He ran a good unit under very difficult circumstances, but the Queen of the hospital was an elderly Christian nurse who gave her whole life to looking after both the buildings and the patients. The President of Bangladesh had given her a medal for it, and it was a real joy to meet such a simple genuine lady who loved the patients because she loved the Lord.

Another major psychiatric hospital stands out in my mind, a huge old-style mental hospital, where one psychiatrist and a medical doctor struggled to keep up standards so that the patients were cared for. I was full of admiration for the way they coped, and the way they utilised what was available to help their patients. They did not have funds or staff for formal occupational therapy but, finding that some of the staff were musical, they organised music therapy sessions, playing to the patients and also teaching them to play. I later visited an equally understaffed hospital in a remote area of Pakistan where the one doctor on the staff coped not only with the mental health patients but also acted as general doctor to the neighbourhood. They seemed unfailingly good humoured and patient as they constantly worked under such great pressure.

At a very isolated Christian hospital in Bangladesh I had a life changing experience. I have never been a small clinic worker, being more comfortable in a hospital setting, however primitive, but I was persuaded to visit a women's centre in a nearby village. I was immediately set on fire by a new understanding of what community work is all about. There was an ordinary village hut, spotlessly clean, containing only local equipment. The women were clean and neat and, after they had been told who I was, one of them asked to speak to me, by interpretation of course. She said, 'Before you people came we were nothing. Our husbands beat us, we were dirty and our children were often sick. Now look at us. Our eyes are bright, our hair is tidy, our husbands respect us and the children are healthy.' I discovered how this had been accomplished. Training courses were made available. Although the women were illiterate they had excellent memories, and had profited by the courses the village workers offered them. They took courses on first aid; good food and how to grow it, clean it and cook it; health care; animal care; child care; simple sanitation, and a lot of other things. At the end of each course there was an oral and practical test, after which they got what they called 'a sustifikit', a piece of paper to hang on the wall. Many of them actually became literate because the short courses made them more confident and acted as an encouragement to go on to literacy. My informant had taken twelve different courses! As I write this 22 years later I still feel the overwhelming excitement of understanding for the first time the importance of aid programmes of this kind. They really accomplished something.

The same applied to some of the programmes in other countries, especially the micro-financial aid in Nepal. For example, one sewing machine could be purchased for a woman who was taught to use it and, when she began to earn money from it, she had to repay the loan by instalments. Once it had been paid back another woman got a sewing machine, or other means of income creation, and so it went on. Because they were all local everyone watched the beneficiary of the loan to ensure she paid her bit back, so that the next person could benefit. On my first 'enlightenment' in Bangladesh I was so excited that I danced along the edge of a rice field, slipped off the mud wall, and got a bad skin loss and subsequent infection of my arm. But it was worth it.

It was an unusual experience for me to be asked to speak to 70 national staff members of a large paper factory on 'How to be a Leader'. I asked to speak by interpretation but they wanted it in English, so I had to concentrate very hard as I chose words that hopefully everyone would understand. The session was made all the harder by the fact that the back of the hall was a through-way for all the workers from the noisy factory room next door. But I plodded on and did my best. This lecture was followed by a session with six doctors on schizophrenia. The outcome was something of a shock. I had been seeing quite a lot of patients for the hospital, and the day after my lecture the paper mill administrators requested that I see some of their people. To our surprise a very large group of men and a few women arrived from the factory. Many of them were migrants from India who had suffered from some form of mental trouble for which they were taking medicine and they all wanted me to see them. The national staff spoke briefly to them all and sorted out the ones I should see, totalling about twelve I think. But we got the rest to line up, I read their papers and said as far as I could see it was good medicine and they should go on with it. I took care to feel the pulse, for that is a very important form of diagnosis in many communities. I then sat down to see the twelve people, each of whom needed about an hour due to interpretation. We all did the best we could to love and care for the people during the long wait and we also took care of ourselves, finding time to eat adequately as the day wore on. I saw a few more the next morning and wished very much that the hospital in which I was based could open a psychiatric department.

It was in overworked situations such as these two days that I found myself increasingly grateful to God for his help. I came to appreciate the help God gave me with the language problem. I frequently found myself in situations where I could not communicate directly with the patients because they did not speak Hindi, Urdu or Nepali. I was dependent on interpretation, but I discovered I could pick up some non-verbal clues by watching them as they told their problem in their own language. There was one patient I remember, in another Asian country, who was a remarkable example of God helping me. She was a middle aged person brought by her husband because he was at his wits' end. She was so agitated that she could hardly eat or sleep and he had to be with her day and night to comfort and help her. They had tried local healers, some Western medicine, and some local medications that were historically valued by the people, but nothing had helped. From my clinical experience I hardly needed to take a history, it was so obvious what was wrong. I heard her story, we checked her physically, and found all was normal, so I put her straight onto medicines that were tranquillising as well as anti-depressant. I asked to see her in three days' time, after which I would be leaving, and could not believe my eyes when she turned up. I think God had speeded up the usually delayed action of the medication, because she was tidy, much quieter and able to sit still, was beginning to sleep better and even managed a smile! I handed over her care to one of the doctors in the hospital and the last I heard she had made excellent progress, and her husband was so relieved and thankful. I really felt that God sent this case to me so that I could demonstrate to staff and patients in the short time I was there that something really could be done to help the mentally sick.

I also began working out the best way to help the missionary community and their leaders. The key was to give some lectures as soon as possible, which gave the audience the chance to look me over and to discover that I did not have two horns and a tail, and that despite the dreaded title 'psychiatrist' I was just an ordinary Christian doctor! The next thing was to work out an appointment system, allocating one and a half hours per person or family group. The third thing was the importance of record keeping. I wrote up every case in a proper clinical format on my portable typewriter, which went everywhere with me in those pre-computer days.

I was very careful about confidentiality. I explained to my patients that I needed to keep records in case they ever wanted to write to me for advice, and reassured them that only I would have access to their records and that I would never give information about them without their permission. This policy worked very well for the next 20 years of both mobile and static ministry. The biggest problem was writing to their mission if it was necessary. I resolved this by discussing the letter with the person concerned and linking it with the importance of getting them properly looked after.

As far as the Mission leaders were concerned, I tried not to be dogmatic or insensitive, realising that they too had heavy and rather lonely jobs, very little office help, too much travelling and usually did not have 'safe' people with whom they could discuss serious local problems. I had very good discussion sessions with many of them and gained from them a lot of very valuable information about missionary care in their organisation. Most of them really wanted to modernise and improve their administrative structures and to move on to new patterns of caring for all aspects of missionary health and welfare. Some years later it was good to meet some of them at conferences which pin-pointed these needs and discussed their resolution.

Bangladesh also taught me how to lecture at conferences. I was asked to be the main speaker at the annual Dacca conference, a formidable proposition indeed. 'Terrified' would be an understatement of how scared I was, but it gave me the opportunity to prepare a series of lectures that would be useful for many years to come, with suitable local modifications, and to learn how to handle speaking several times in a large conference. I discovered that 'de-gassed' cola was a wonderful drink between sessions, and many times saw some kind lady vigorously stirring a glass with a fork to get the bubbles out, and thus prevent me burping in the middle of my next talk!

As you may imagine I very often said to myself on this first tour, 'Can it be me?' I was deeply grateful to God for his help. I was having to learn how to do it and breaking a lot of new ground. He helped me establish a pattern that could be transferred to other places and showed me how to fulfil both the commissions he had given me, the lectures in simple psychiatry and caring for missionaries. I was thankful that he had restored me to health, and given me power to stand up and talk before all sorts of audiences, with or without an interpreter. People told me I spoke so simply and clearly that they could understand and I made it my ambition to learn how to put complicated matters into simple sentences. My stammer was there but did not seem to affect my work and in fact I rarely thought of it unless I heard my own recordings! I handled that by not listening to them – and if I felt I was getting a bit stressed-out, which made my stammer worse, I just took some time off! But I often asked myself, 'Am I really standing up and giving four major conference addresses in a large hall full of missionaries? Is it really me mixing constantly with strangers, moving on from one group to another and rarely meeting a person I know?' Sometimes I could hardly believe it and was so grateful to God for his calling and empowerment – and for the sheer enjoyment I got out of doing this work. I was not, of course, always successful. Some lectures were a total flop, and some patients did not like me a bit, but that's life, so I just picked myself up and tried to do better next time. Like anyone else I could feel bad-tempered on occasions, but I learned to deal with it by going out to the market or a local park – and my love of birdwatching stood me in good stead. I was also very glad that I was comparatively old, single, small and female! In my generation these characteristics were not particularly valued, although the modern world thinks differently about some of them, but I found they really helped me. I was a threat to nobody.

I was also very grateful that God had taught me to live an independent spiritual life with him during my many years of heavy load-bearing in India. Because I was mobile I had little opportunity of regular church support, so I was glad I had learned how to keep my spiritual life alive and active. As I mentioned earlier, ever since I became a Christian I have read and marked my Bible, using concordances to help me. I am also in the habit of reading a little book called Daily Light. I learned that in times of pressure, one verse in the mind could keep me going as I thought about it while rushing to the next job. I really knew we were in partnership, that God had called me to the job and that I was right to take it just as it came. All I had to do was to obey, keep on learning and always to look to him for power.

My other great support was the communion table. I had always found this a place for re-cementing my relationship with God and during my very busy hospital years I followed a pattern that Amy Carmichael had developed many years previously in Dohnavur, South India. She was more or less bedridden, and used to have daily communion on her own with her breakfast toast and tea, using the words of the church service. I did the same when I was delayed in hospital and could not go to church. I set out a table and prayed the communion prayers, and using toast and tea shared the church communion from my room. I did this regularly when I was travelling and although this practice may shock some Christians, I felt quite at peace about it and benefited greatly from it.

I also learnt that if I was to continue in this role I needed to plan clear holiday time, when I could unwind, rest and be renewed for the next task. At intervals my family would come to join me wherever I was, so that we could have fun together. I have no idea where the money came from, but obviously God provided enough

My brother and sister-in-law join me on holiday in Nepal

for these wonderful holidays. My first visitors in my mobile life were my brother and sister-in-law who joined me for a holiday in Nepal and we had many adventures. One wonderful Christmas when I was again in Nepal my sister came. We had a memorable time together, staying in a lovely hotel in Pokhra on the edge of the lake. We ate Christmas dinner in an extraordinary restaurant that gathered up stray foreigners and we ate a very odd multinational meal. Our bedroom was part of a circular house, like a huge cake of which we had one slice, and we woke every morning to the sight of the high snowy peaks. One day I got up rather early and went out. I saw something wonderful, rushed back into the bedroom and said, 'Vicky, you *must* get up *now* and come outside'. A flock of scarlet minivet birds had settled just outside our house and were fluttering up and down against a magnificent backdrop of the high snow-peaked Himalayas. A marvellous Christmas present from God.

But before the holidays began there was more travelling to do. I left Bangladesh with regret. During my stay I had visited seven different centres, and deeply appreciated all that people had taught me. I retained a picture of once despised women neatly dressed, going to work in Dacca stitching shirts in the Van Heusen factory, and becoming respected and valued as wage earners. I remembered the joy of the people at being politically free and prayed that this might be translated into the spiritual freedom and joy the Lord wanted them to have. And I remembered the many wonderful missionaries I met, the problems they faced in family care and overall welfare, the need for outside roles and friends for otherwise rather housebound wives, and the heavy work loads and lonely lives some of the single women experienced. As I got on the plane to move on to India again, I saluted them for their cheerfulness, dedication and resilience, and humbly prayed that I might do better myself.

# 9

# An extension of my commission

On arrival in India I spent a few days in a BMMF Mission conference, and in the middle of it I felt that God was asking me to be prepared to go out of Asia for a wider ministry. In my morning Bible study I had read, 'Trust in the Lord with all your heart and do not rely on your own understanding. In everything acknowledge him and he will direct your paths', so I immediately told the Lord I was willing to extend if that was what he wanted. I was surprised how fast he worked. One of the speakers mentioned my work in her plenary talk and indicated I might be available to other countries. This led to immediate invitations to USA, Australia and New Zealand. I also accepted an invitation to tour the Emmanuel Hospital Association hospitals in India, which would be a three month assignment. It was then obvious to me that my travelling role would extend for a further two years at least and I was content to take this from God's hand.

After a few days in North India I went down by train to a marvellous South Indian Christian hospital. This was a wonderful opportunity to see the South Indian Christians in action, directed by a most dedicated doctor. The outcome was a dream come true. The young doctor who acted as my interpreter was so enthused by psychiatry that he went off and got his training and there is now a flourishing psychiatric department in the hospital. I was really excited to play a small part in this, for I was firmly committed to the current pattern of hospitals run by the national churches or a local board of managers in whom control was vested and which had a vision for development of the services offered.

I was also stimulated by an extra job the Director did on Sundays. He invited street boys to his home, where he had fixed up a huge bathing tub in which they could soak. He had a store of clothes, so they washed the ones they were wearing and put on a clean set which they wore till they came back next week. After food, games and a Bible talk and prayer, off they went for another week of homelessness and the dangers of living on the street. He also opened a bank for them and if they contributed a small amount he doubled it, so they had every incentive to try to save a few coins. This, however, was one of the times I failed to meet expectations. He suddenly asked me to give a talk to the boys, and quite honestly I did not feel I could do it. I knew nothing of their lives and backgrounds and so did not take it on. I have always wished I had trusted God a bit more and thought of some simple thing I could have said!

After that it was time for me to leave. I had given ten lectures, a chapel talk and seen 37 somewhat complicated patients, and have long remembered my time there as very special. I got on the train for Madras and next day went to Delhi, a very long journey. I stayed there for nine days resting and recuperating and then set off for Pakistan. I took the train to the border, walking over and getting on the Pakistan train on the other side. I could not help remembering the massacres on these trains as Indians and Pakistanis crossed over to reach their own countries after Independence, but all was pleasant and peaceful by the time I crossed. Finally we reached the lovely historic city of Lahore. There I followed the familiar pattern of giving lectures to church groups, missionaries and other groups, visiting the local psychiatric hospitals and seeing patients or those with problems they wished to discuss. I met with some of the mission leaders and began to increase my knowledge of expatriate problems. I also had the chance to do some sightseeing, well worth while in such a lovely city, and was privileged to meet a famous Pakistani woman doctor who was the only child psychiatrist in Pakistan at that time.

The main purpose of my time in Pakistan was to spend three months living in the hills. I would be involved with two groups, the language students who were new to the country and established missionaries who rented houses to be near their children's boarding schools. I moved up to Murree on 30 April and was given a nice bedroom and a separate room for seeing people in a house called Hill Lodge. This was a large rambling place with rather small quarters for the students, and a noise and smell problem with flying foxes which nested in the roof.

Nobody in Murree knew much about me and I realised again that the word 'psychiatrist' aroused the deepest suspicions. So

I decided to spend most of my time in the garden watching the birds, while the students watched me! I gradually made friends and we all settled down together. I used some of the time to visit missionaries in their locations, going, for example, to a well-known Mission Hospital at Bannu and to the rather dirty town of Rawalpindi just down the mountain from Murree. After that, things settled down into the pattern of lectures to expatriates and various other groups, individual consultations and finally speaking at the annual spiritual life conference. An interesting spin-off was experiencing the annual month-long Muslim fast. We continued to eat in our own home, but out of respect did not eat or drink anything in public during the fasting hours. I remember sitting at a table in the bazaar, having just returned from Rawalpindi, and looking at bottles of water placed before us. When the gun went off to signal the end of the fast, everyone produced paper bags and bottles of water and the evening rejoicing began. The people made a special sort of strengthening soup and invited friends to share it.

God used a holiday in a wild and remote part of Pakistan to help me with a problem. As I have previously indicated I have never been any good at evangelism and it has always worried me. During the holiday it came to a head, for one of our party was a real old style evangelist and I saw her at work. This aroused all my own anxieties and inferiorities until one morning I went outside to a bean field, which was our only toilet. While I was there I began to think of my evangelistic difficulties and to ask God to help me. As clear as anything God put into my mind the knowledge that if he had wanted me to be an evangelist he would have gifted me with the power to do so. But he had other work for me to do and it was time I stopped moaning about my own inadequacies. So I stood up in the middle of the bean field and said to God, 'Okay, if you have not enabled me to be an evangelist I will stop moaning and take from you the gifts you give me for the ministry to which you have called me'. After that I felt happier and much more confident that 'there are diversities of gifts but the same Spirit', ie we do not all have the same job.

I was very grateful for this very interesting holiday which had an unexpected sequel. One Sunday evening towards the end of our stay we were sitting under a tree resting when a few local women came along in their colourful tribal dress. We had been singing some hymns and choruses and to our surprise one of the women suddenly joined in, using her own language. It emerged that a man had stayed with the group for some weeks doing a research programme and he used to sing hymns as he worked, and the local people had picked them up. Months later the woman we had met, and her husband, came down to Delhi to help with language translation and she appeared wearing jeans and a T shirt, much to my surprise!

In August it was time to pack up and move on. I made a brief return to Nur Manzil where all was well and then flew on to Kathmandu, Nepal. It was lovely to be back. I worked for my old mission, United Mission to Nepal, and also for the International Nepal Fellowship. My visit lasted until April 1983 and I travelled widely over large sections of the country. I used planes, buses, cars, and feet as I went to towns, villages, isolated hilltop agricultural projects, hydroelectric dams and many other locations. The strangest place in which I ever gave lectures, after the Paper Mill in Bangladesh, was beside a blackboard in the middle of a cornfield in inland Nepal, a lovely experience, with the birds competing for my attention in quite a serious way. But I managed to hold on to my psychiatric lecture. I was, of course, delighted to visit Tansen where everything was going fine. Ingeborg and I had a great reunion. Every visit followed the same pattern of lectures suitable to the area, many discussions with nationals and expatriates about their problems, discussions with project leaders and sometimes seeing national patients. One of my outstanding memories is of going to visit a rather isolated hospital in the mountains. We had a long walk and, after sleeping in a trailside inn, started off again early next morning. We were climbing up a hill when the sun rose on the huge snow mountains towering over a lower peak. As we reached the top we suddenly saw perched on a branch against the snowy background, a brilliant red bird called the flame-coloured bulbul. It was breathtaking.

Another wonderful experience was going to a place in the remote Northwest. I could not get on the regular daily flight, so my hosts the United Mission to Nepal finally chartered a United Nations plane to take a load of freight and asked them to take me with them as the only passenger. The pilot was devoted to his grandmother and immediately adopted me. After we took off he said, 'What would you like to see?' Never thinking it would be possible I said, 'Could we go as close to Annapurna as possible?' 'No problem' he said, and proceeded to give me a private guided tour of the four peaks. When we landed I gave him the biggest kiss he had ever had from an old lady, kissing not being much of a Nepali custom, and he was very pleased indeed. Even now, 20 years later, the thought of what I saw gives me goose pimples of excitement and pleasure.

This remote place taught me much about missionary resilience. It was a wonderful location, but tough going domestically. Wood stoves were used which gave off a black smoke due to the oil content, so everyone wore black clothes and their skins turned black however hard they washed. My bedroom was over the cow shed, so placed in order to share the warmth that came off the cattle, but the smell was something else. There were missionary children on site being educated by an expatriate teacher appointed to UMN for that purpose, and they took the whole thing in their stride. A small church was growing and the professional aspect of the work, although sometimes hard going, was very satisfying. Through a college which they had created, training in agriculture and other local needs such as veterinary care was given and I was greatly impressed with everything I saw both there and in all the other locations I visited. I was very happy to be back in Nepal, but was also full of thankfulness that I could be there without the old painful yearning to stay, for I knew that God had taught me much and had moved me on.

In another remote place I had the interesting experience of talking with a local healer, one of my friends interpreting when I got stuck. He was an illiterate man and said he had not wanted to be a healer, because it was a painful business. But one day walking in the forest he felt God calling him to take up this work. So he stayed four days alone in the forest preparing himself to receive the spirit that would come when he was trying to heal. This meant going into a trance and it was the trance experience that caused him real pain, although he could not describe it clearly. All he could tell us was that he dreaded being asked to heal for it meant personal pain, but he felt sure that was what God wanted him to do. He did not charge money for his services but the locals fed him and gave him clothes, and he went on doing part-time small scale farming. What really impressed us was the pain of the work and my friend explained to him the pain Jesus had suffered as he died for our sins on the cross, and that he also became exhausted during his earthly ministry. I have never heard any more about this man but have continued to pray for him. Later on, a group of Christian medical workers in Nepal began to conduct classes in simple medical diagnosis for traditional healers. The aim was that by working together they could help more people – if the healer spotted a treatable illness he could advise them to go to the hospital, and because he said so, they would not be frightened to come to a place where methods were unfamiliar. One day I happened to see the healers arrive for their weekly classes, many covered in feathers and carrying traditional equipment, which was left outside the door when they went inside. The staff would conduct classes on various medical conditions and, at the end of the day, if the healers wished, the staff would pray with them, asking Jesus to give them spiritual and medical understanding, wise judgement and a genuine desire to help their patients. The same sort of thing is being done in parts of Africa, and much prayer goes up for these people as they attend their seminars. Some are frauds of course, but others are as genuine as my friend from the high Nepali mountain where I met him.

Overall, I found that much was developing in Nepal. UMN was engaged in a large number of projects ranging from hospitals and schools to large scale hydroelectric projects, agriculture and veterinary science. Local people were being taught skills by which they could increase their income, using only what was available locally. As nationals became trained and experienced, more and more Nepali people were occupying responsible positions in UMN work, although in things like hydroelectric constructions this would take several more years to accomplish. The church was growing rapidly. In the early days it was non-denominational, being simply The Nepali Church, but that changed later on when Nepali Christians who had returned from other countries, or foreigners, introduced denominationalism.

By this time I had collected a great deal of material about missionary mental health needs, and the availability of help should it be required. All in all, I felt missionaries were doing very well although there were a few locations where stress levels seemed much higher than in other areas. I began to think about possible reasons for this, but shelved much of it in the back of my mind until I had more leisure to study it effectively. The immediate conclusion I reached was that generally speaking missionary service is both an enjoyable experience and a high stress occupation! I continued to keep very careful records and decided that when I had an opportunity I would see if I could analyse these and draw some conclusions.

When I went home for a break in 1983 I realised that the expanded pattern God had shown me was about to begin. I had consultations with all the BMMF offices in the UK, during which I shared some of the facts and figures about missionary mental health and well-being that I had collected. I remained very grateful for the support they gave me and the encouragement to go wherever God was leading. I was also, of course, instructed to take a holiday, which I did, for I am 100% convinced of the importance of not only working hard but also of taking adequate time off.

In the Autumn I set off nervously for my first experience of working in Canada and the USA. I need not have been nervous for they were all wonderful to me and I learned a great deal while I was there. One of my major memories was a big Christian university where I was to speak about missions in general. It was truly daunting, a huge lecture room full of young students. In the front row was a large coloured lady who was enthusiastic about everything, and we

An opportunity to visit the White House during a visit to the USA

had not been going long before she chipped in with 'Hallelujah, that's right sister, preach on', and 'That's right sister, sock it to them!' She continued as my 'cheer leader' till the end of the talk. The authorities then said they wanted me to repeat the talk next day because they had not taped it and I said it would be impossible without the coloured lady! However, I had to speak into a dull microphone, with no audience stimulation, and I do not think the recorded version was much good.

The important thing in Canada and the States was the people I met. I found I had colleagues, people who had been involved in home-based mental health care of missionaries for many years, so we had a great deal to talk about. I made friends for life, meeting many of the 'greats' in the Christian mental health world. I was very pleased to be asked to attend a conference called *Mental Health and Missions*, people attending by invitation only. This remained a very important link and, as it gradually expanded, it was opened up to anyone wishing to come. 21 years later I was honoured to be asked to give the closing plenary session of the 25th anniversary conference in 2004.

The title they gave me was *'Well done good and faithful servant'*. I was touched by the care they took of me. When I was due to go on the platform a man came up to me, offered me his arm and said, 'Will you walk the walk?' I am a part-time historian, and in the UK this phrase would be used when prisoners went to execution, or when sailors had to walk the plank to their deaths! I realised, however, that in my case it was their kind way of making sure their 83 year old speaker got on the platform without falling down.

To return to 1984, before I set off again for Pakistan I decided to ask All Souls Church in Langham Place, London, if I could become a church member and be recognised as one of their commissioned missionaries. I had been rather vaguely in touch since the end of my time at Nur Manzil but it had never been properly formalised. I was very glad when they accepted me and linked me up with two fellowship groups that would pray for me regularly and help me if I had any needs. This link has remained strong ever since and is another thing for which I constantly thank God. They are endlessly kind to me.

Another thing that happened in this short time at home was of profound importance for the future. Stanley Davies of Evangelical Missionary Alliance, now Global Connections, arranged a day seminar for people interested in missionary mental health, and gave me the whole day to use as I thought best. We expected about 30 people, but in the end 85 came and I was able to spread out in simple statistics the early findings based on my case work, plus some material on the types of stress that appeared most prevalent in the missionary community. After I had flown off for my second visit to Pakistan a committee was formed to discuss how better mental health care could be offered to missionaries, which later on led to the development of a new missionary mental health service in England, a partner to the one already established in Scotland.

Pakistan was a busy round of visits to seven different centres, resulting in 82 lectures to a variety of groups, 66 psychiatric consultations, and informal meetings with both nationals and the missionary community. The major thing I remember is the splendid group of Far Eastern missionaries who attended all my lectures, and were both dedicated and intelligent. I lived in a large room in the cathedral guest house and it was a real help to have a familiar place to retire to in my short intervals between assignments.

My next visit to India was very interesting. I worked initially with the Indian community in Calcutta. They were setting up a project for rehabilitation of mentally ill patients and wanted me to inspect the programme and give them some advice about how to proceed. I thoroughly enjoyed this time and was delighted to revisit this wonderful, maddening, sprawling, historic city. My major project, however, was to live in the Landour hills with language students and missionaries on holiday. The work followed the usual pattern of interviewing missionaries and nationals when requested, and giving lectures on mental health topics. Once again I was the main speaker at the annual conference.

The only snag was my accommodation. I was given a nice little house beside the tennis court. This had two rooms, one my office-cum-bedroom and the other the place where I could see

Working in Landour near the language school.
My bedroom and office were over an open drain!

people who asked for appointments. Unfortunately the house was built over an open drain, and the smell became rather unpleasant after the cook had finished preparing meals and doing the washing up. However, we were able to get most of the drain covered over, which reduced the smell, and I really enjoyed my time there.

In writing about these visits they seem almost predictable in pattern, but in reality were endlessly fascinating. The cultural aspects of mental health needs changed from country to country, and from expatriate to expatriate. While not neglecting formal psychiatric examination, and entry into people's spiritual experiences when they invited me in, I found it very important to explore and discuss the social and occupational aspects of my patients' lives. Social isolation, overwork, workaholism and fractured interpersonal relationships were obviously extremely important aspects of missionary mental health care, and later on I was to be glad I had taken such careful notes of these matters.

My time in India was not all work. When I returned from the hills I attended a BMMF conference in South India and then met my sister in Madras for a wonderful holiday in the famous South Indian hill station called Ootacamund (Ooty for short). Later in life I became a TV fan of snooker (a kind of billiards) and was delighted to have seen the original snooker tables in Ooty where the game was created – and to have read the correspondence with Mr Gladstone, the Prime Minister in UK, about the new invention. We had a very amusing time in Ooty and enjoyed ourselves hugely apart from one night. A pop group was given the room next door, about seven people all packed in and, because of rain, their concert was cancelled. So they played and smoked in their room all night, and left early in the morning without paying their bill! The weather was terribly wet and cold during our first week, so we spent a lot of time in bed playing board games and reading, which was very good for both of us. When the rain finally stopped we opened our door to find the local wild horses had all gathered on our verandah for shelter, making a huge mess everywhere. But nothing could stop us laughing and enjoying each other's company.

Finally Vicky had to go back home and I had to get on with my programme. Before I had finalised my contract with BMMF to return overseas, I had been told that the Emmanuel Hospital Association (EHA) would like me to visit all their work in India. I was delighted to do this, because I was very supportive of their principles of operation. EHA was created when several mission hospitals, for various valid reasons, were possibly going to have to close. EHA was created to take these hospitals on and staff them with predominantly national staff, expatriates working under Indian management as teachers and consultants in various specialities. The big change was that ownership was now vested in the Indian people, not overseas mission groups. It has not been easy but they have prospered and the work is a force for good in many parts of India. I personally learned a lot, met many fine people, and gave many lectures, seminars and patient consultations. Courage was my major impression of the staff working in EHA hospitals. It was not always easy but they plodded on with faith and determination.

I visited nine EHA hospitals, breaking off in the middle to give some lectures to language school students in Nepal, all new missionaries. Right at the end I was back in my flat in Delhi when a lady I knew came rushing over to tell me that Mrs Gandhi, the Prime Minister, had been shot by her Sikh guards. Expecting trouble, the local Sikh community began shutting up their shops, so we all rushed round to purchase supplies before they left. It was as well they did leave, for their stores were all burned down that night. My problem was that I had to go to the airport to catch a flight to Manila, where I was to attend a conference. I asked a friend if he could take me to the airport in the early afternoon when Mrs Gandhi was being cremated in the other side of Delhi from the airport. This would enable us to go there before the crowds came back, with the possibility of further violence. I had to wait for over ten hours for my flight. The airport was full of Sikhs leaving the country till things settled down. It never entered my head that food and drink could run out, but seeing evidence that supplies would not last I immediately bought water, cakes and chocolate. After a long and rather tense wait I got the flight, and settled back into my economy seat with a *huge* bottle of water and some proper food.

Manila was the start of a new addition to my work. It was one of the first ever world conferences on '*Mental Health of Missionaries*' and I was privileged to be asked to give a paper. It was a wonderful time. We had cut-price accommodation in a first class hotel and, after some of the privations I had experienced in my travels, it was bliss indeed to have a real bath and to eat some first class food. The enthusiasm and fellowship were amazing, and it was a marvellous academic and spiritual banquet. Friendships were made that have lasted to the present day. I had been asked to write some articles on missionary stress for an American missionary journal called *Evangelical Missions Quarterly (EMQ)*. I eventually turned out nine articles, and ultimately made them the basis for my book *Honourably Wounded*, about which I have written further below. I discovered that they had been a help to people at the conference, which encouraged me to continue taking careful notes on missionary stress which I would need when I later began a formal research programme. We regretted the conference coming to an end but it was a good thing it did. Shortly after we left, terrorists burned our hotel down. Later I bumped into a lady at an airport who had been in the hotel when the fire broke out who told me of the difficulty they experienced getting to safety.

On return to India I finished my EHA assignment, completed my articles, took a holiday and added up my 1984 statistics: 179

lectures, 21 religious talks, 154 new patients, 27 follow ups and 42 professional discussions, so not a bad year's work. People asked me why I kept statistics. The reason is that I have an enquiring mind, and like to analyse my work to see whether principles are emerging that may be useful. In addition, there are inherent dangers in working alone in an unstructured kind of job and some sort of check needs to be made that work is actually being done and hopefully something accomplished. Although I was responsible to BMMF, and to EHA or whoever had asked me to come, I also felt it important to be responsible to myself, to keep good records, to review what I was doing and see what could be improved or should be dropped entirely. I have operated on this system ever since and find it keeps me on course in my rather odd ministry. I also conduct a spiritual audit at the end of the year, thinking about what I have learnt. At the same time I ask God to give me a verse for the coming year, and I re-commit myself to him for whatever he has on plan. I find these periods of reflection and re-commitment very valuable. I often have very little idea what the next year may hold, so it is helpful to hand it back to God to look after and to ask him for the power to carry out whatever the ministry turns out to be.

In February 1985 I was called to the Foreigners Registration Office in Delhi. Missionaries now had to get a visa to work in India, and they wanted to know what I was doing. I explained I was in personnel care, and that I had meetings booked until April, and they kindly allowed me to stay to complete the work. 'But', they said sternly, 'you must go by April'. So I completed my EHA work, wound everything up, dismantled my flat and prepared to go. Interestingly enough, the worst cultural mistake I ever made was on the day I was leaving India. A man I knew well came to say goodbye. I was in hot weather clothes, and had put my feet on a stool while relaxing with a cool drink. When my friend had his drink and we sat down, without thinking I put my feet back on the stool so that the soles faced him. In a flash I remembered that this is very rude behaviour in India, took my feet down and apologised. 'Well', he said, 'I minded, but then I remembered you are only a poor foreigner anyway!' We both laughed, but it was strange to be reminded I was still a foreigner after 35 years in India and Nepal! But it was true that basically I felt British, not Indian, and could not wait to see my own homeland despite my sincere love of my Asian foster-countries.

# 10

# A new pattern and a new job

On arrival home in 1985 I went up to my lovely rooms in Scotland, resting and recuperating, entertaining family and friends and generally unwinding. I needed it by that time, but the lovely countryside, fishing the lake, walking in the hills and generally switching off work were just what the doctor ordered! When I was rested I began thinking over what I was to do next. I realised that I was now on a different track. I was totally committed to caring for missionaries and knew that this was what God wanted me to concentrate on, rather than combining it with teaching in rural hospitals.

Throughout 1985 my new pattern of work developed rapidly. Within the UK I had a heavy programme of meeting mission officials and doctors interested in missionary health care, attending professional conferences as part of my own continuing medical education programme, conducting seminars with several missions, and discussing a new venture that was hopefully going to start in 1986. This was going to be another dream come true. As I previously described, following my day-seminar on Missionary Mental Health a committee was formed to discuss the issues of suitable missionary health care, including mental health as a separate entity in the programme. As a result they were offered a suitable venue for a new venture. The famous Mildmay Mission Hospital in South London had been taken over by the British National Health Service, which finally decided to close it. However, two women went in every week to keep it clean, and to pray that God would reopen it in its original form as a Christian hospital for the needy in the area. He heard and answered their prayers and a plan was devised to reopen the Mildmay Hospital to provide a health care service for the local community. The new

Board of the Mildmay heard of our need for a place to care for missionary health and, since this had been part of the old role before the hospital closed, they felt it right to offer us rooms rent free where we could open the missionary service. Dr Veronica Moss, who was already physician to a large mission, was asked to be half-time physician and director of the new missionary unit, becoming director of the Mildmay programme in the other half of her time. I was approached and asked to open the psychiatric section, which would also be half-time work. We planned to open the unit in October 1986. I asked Veronica and the board if I could periodically work full weeks instead of half, thus freeing me to continue my short-term work overseas. They were in full agreement and said I could arrange it any way I wanted so long as I fulfilled my work-agreement each year – and that I was not away for too long at any one time. They also told me I would get a salary for my work, which was very nice to hear! We called the clinic Missionary and Volunteers Health Service, later renamed Interhealth, and were linked in fellowship with similar groups in Scotland and the North of England.

While waiting for the new Mildmay work to start, I accepted another invitation to the USA. This lasted for nearly a month, and involved an extensive tour of the many people interested in missionary mental health, as well as giving relevant seminars and lectures. Because I was accustomed to lecturing to people who spoke moderate or poor English, I had developed a simple style of speaking, and even in a sophisticated well-educated country like America I found this very useful when lecturing to non-medical groups. I was happy to meet the editor of the *Evangelical Missions Quarterly* who was publishing my articles on missionary stress. It seemed strange to see the simple things which I began writing on a battered typewriter in Bangladesh printed in a prestigious Christian journal.

I have always enjoyed working in America and the friendliness of the people. This friendliness took a quantum leap forward when I was using the kerb-side check-in at Philadelphia airport. An enormous porter helped me with my luggage and I gave him the usual tip. He suddenly said, 'May I kiss you?' 'Certainly', I said, and was picked up and kissed very heartily, much to my bewilderment. My friend told me afterwards I had probably given him ten dollars rather than one dollar because all the notes are the same colour! Still, it was a nice experience. I met another very interesting man on an aircraft, a huge football player. He was having a difference of opinion with his manager and, when he read the Bible, he felt God was telling him to discuss this with a friend, so that was what he was going to do. He was so big there was no way he could occupy only one seat, and I was being slowly compressed to the point of permanent damage. Ultimately the hostess gave him three seats to himself. He was a lovely person and I greatly enjoyed his company.

These personal encounters were a constant source of pleasure to me as I travelled. As I got older I was more and more able to chat to people and I often ended up having a mini-counselling or short prayer session. People were endlessly kind. I once got stranded in a small US airport, and the cabin attendant was so worried about me he would not leave until someone turned up to collect me. He also gave me a first class toilet bag in case I had any needs! Another Good Samaritan was a Government official going on assignment to Canada. We all had to change planes at Boston and, instead of going off to his big meeting, he insisted on helping two of us, one elderly (me) and one disabled, and would not leave us till he had handed us over to a sympathetic check-in person with the request to take special care of us. On one glorious occasion British Airways came to the rescue when I had a long flight ahead of me. I was not feeling particularly well – nothing serious, just general fatigue. I got talking to the ticket man about my long years of flying BA, always cheapest economy of course, and he suddenly stopped talking and began telephoning, leaving me standing there not knowing what was going on. When he put the phone down he handed me a Business class ticket, a marvellous upgrade from God! So I simply went to bed for the whole long flight and felt fine on arrival.

I have often remembered incidents in India when I felt God had a real hand in the relationships I made with people while travelling. Such personal encounters helped to make the journeys enjoyable, although I occasionally had a few unpleasant ones but was never harmed. One of the pleasant experiences was in a first class sleeper compartment on an Indian train, which I shared with a very nice Indian businessman who had family problems. We talked about them for some time and, when I got into my bunk, I prayed silently for him before I slept. Next morning he was getting off the train before me, and while saying goodbye he added 'Please remember to pray for me as you did last night'. How he knew I have no idea, for I had not been visibly praying!

One of the most unusual encounters I had was in Nepal. I

was walking up a huge stone staircase at the start of the Tansen trail. This took four hours to get up and I was only half way through when it began to get dark, and I had left my torch with the man carrying my bag who was a good way behind me. Suddenly round the corner behind me came a soldier, obviously very drunk, and my heart sank. But I need not have worried. The thing he remembered in his drunken state was that the British Army had told him to be kind to women in distress! So he asked politely if he might take my hand, and we walked hand in hand up the rest of the trail till we reached an inn. He told the women who ran it to take good care of me and then staggered off up the hill. I think he had probably been holding my hand more to keep himself upright than to help me! Finally my porter turned up extremely anxious to know I was okay. I enjoyed such personal moments because they were funny and they also reminded me that God was indeed looking after me.

It was now October 1986 and time to start work at the Missionary and Volunteers Health Service in the Mildmay Hospital. I duly turned up to inspect my new office. I had a table, two chairs, a desk with my own typewriter on it (before I became computer literate) and a filing cabinet. I also had one-twelfth of a secretary. The only snag was I had no patients. There had never been a dedicated psychiatric service available for missionaries and there was obviously reluctance to use it. Veronica sent me a few patients and I had a few selection interviews to do, but clearly the service needed to be explained to the people for whom it was created. So I decided to go calling. I went to see the heads of many missions and explained that we were setting up a service for missionaries at the Mildmay Hospital. This would include the usual physical care missionaries received and also a psychological service. We could offer psychological selection interviews, in-service psychological care and advice to missionaries returning on furlough, and assistance during final resettlement in their home countries. In addition we would be very interested in discussing missionary care with home office mission staff. These visits were very interesting, ranging from traditional British mission offices to a large Roman Catholic training college for ordained priests preparing for overseas service. Gradually the work built up, and ultimately I had more than enough to do. At the end of our first full year, 505 patients had attended for physical examination and 143 for psychological help or preliminary screening, with 122 follow up sessions. In the 'other half of my life', I had visited Ecuador,

Holland, Morocco and Germany – and done a good deal of work in UK. So it had been a very satisfying first year.

Veronica had been very busy with both the missionary unit and the growing work in the Mildmay hospital itself. After a few years she decided she must give up the missionary care section and concentrate on the expanding hospital work, which was just about to open the care for HIV/AIDS patients which has made it world famous. We heard that Dr Ted Lankester might be interested in replacing her as physician and head of the missionary unit, and have been very grateful to God that he joined us. We missed Veronica very much, but realised God had new plans in store. Ted was just the person to take on the further development of the missionary clinic, later known as Interhealth. He had a large experience of medical work in India, and was an energetic, gifted person and a grand colleague. We moved out of our downstairs rooms to a unit on the top floor which I liked very much, and settled down happily to our ever-expanding work.

The next few years were very busy. My travels took me to many countries where I usually gave a whole series of lectures in a conference setting. An entry in my passport when I lectured in Singapore amused me for many years to come: 'Dr Marjory Foyle is permitted to perform in Singapore'. Apparently one had to get an entertainment licence to give lectures! Everywhere I went I continued to give private interviews on request.

During my time at Interhealth I was also busy writing. I had heard that the EMQ articles on missionary stress had been appreciated, so decided to expand them into a book which I called *Honourably Wounded*, subtitled *Stress among Christian Workers*. This was published in 1987, and later translated into German, French, Korean and Chinese. A few years later, when I had gathered a lot of new material, I prepared the second edition of *Honourably Wounded*, published in 2001. I rewrote it completely, added several new chapters and generally modernised it.

The book dealt with missionary stress, although many of the chapters were also relevant to non-missionaries. It included chapters on depression, interpersonal relations, family, marital and child-related problems, occupational stress and other similar topics. The title was carefully chosen. In older generations, mental health problems were frequently put down to lack of spiritual commitment, prayer or Bible reading. Sometimes the dreaded term 'spiritual backsliding' cropped up. This attitude changed of course, but sometimes serving missionaries did question whether their symptoms were due to personal failure of some kind. During consultations for stress-related problems several missionaries said to me, 'I am afraid to go home because the church will think I am backsliding and anyway I feel like a total failure'. Occasionally this may have been so, but usually there was another reason which I was keen to get over to missions and supporting churches. Soldiers in battle get wounded and, in some countries, are treated with great honour and receive a medal for their wounds. God's servants are also in a battle against evil and they get wounded in the process, physical or psychological symptoms being one of the commonest manifestations. In God's eyes they are certainly not failures. They have usually made heroic efforts to cope, and God sees them as 'the honourably wounded', worthy of medals for gallantry. So at one point I advised the churches to 'polish the organ and bring out the trumpets to welcome God's honourably wounded home!'

As I have already indicated at the end of chapter seven, one of my long standing problems had been the need for housing. Naturally I had prayed much about it, for although my family were more than generous in offering me hospitality I felt it was an imposition on their private lives, and so began to pray even harder. One day my brother, my sister-in-law and I went to a drinks party down the road. There I met a man who was a Christian and ran a housing association to help people needing homes. He told me who to apply to, and I did it the next day.

After some months I was offered what was called 'shared ownership' in quite a nice road – 'shared' meaning I purchased what I could afford and paid rent on the rest. I ended up owning half and renting the other half. I was allocated a lovely top floor flat but, after being there for half an hour, realised I had a problem. It was noisy due to pop music and other things. This was the last thing I wanted and, after several years, I began to pray hard that God would rehouse me. One day in church, in total despair, I said to the Lord with great respect, 'You promised me that if I gave up lands and housing and family you would repay it all a hundredfold. I don't want 100 houses, I only want one. Will you please give me just one and keep the 99 for someone else?' That night my brother rang me and asked if I knew that The Sheppard Trust, a housing project for elderly ladies of limited income, was remodelling their property into flats. I immediately went round and stood opposite a lovely Georgian house in a beautiful area and prayed that this might be my home. I was interviewed and within three months

My wonderful house.
I live on the top floor

was settled in a wonderful flat high in the treetops, opposite where the BMMF office had once been.

I still live in the same place. I am free to live a fully independent life, knowing that help of all kinds is available should I need it. I have two rooms, kitchen and bathroom, laundry facilities, emergency alarms and everything else I need. My back window looks over a lovely garden in which I have a plot of land and, for the first time in my life, I can grow flowers. I tend it like a new born baby! All summer I am down there around 7 a.m. with a cup of tea, when I tend the new blooms and talk to my plants, just like Prince Charles, as well as carrying out the never ending slug and snail watch that a London garden demands. The house management is very caring and understands my desire to continue in voluntary work for as long as I am fit enough. I remain so grateful to God that I moved in a few months before my much loved sister-in-law died, for she was very happy to be well enough to see my new flat and advise me on curtains etc. Because I now lived only ten minutes away from my brother's home I was able to help him after his wife's death and, later on, to look after him when he became rather frail and finally died.

To return to my work at Interhealth, Ted and I discussed my retirement and we agreed that I should go when I reached 70 years of age in November 1991. We therefore began to look for a successor and God sent Dr Ruth Fowke, a well known and experienced psychiatrist, to take over the department. In addition, he sent us Dr Evelyn Sharpe, a lovely friend and a gifted psychiatrist, who remains there to this day. Many others have joined the staff in various capacities and God has truly blessed the whole of the Interhealth work in its new premises in Waterloo Road, London. To me, perhaps one of the best things is the extension of the original work to include cooperative work with secular aid agencies, which involves a sharing of knowledge with the growing number of groups dedicated to helping expatriate volunteers.

When my retirement date arrived, the Interhealth staff arranged a wonderful farewell cum happy birthday party. A few days later I packed up my things and, for once in my life not crying as I said goodbye, returned home to see what God wanted next. To my surprise this included a return to research. When I had finished writing *Honourably Wounded* I realised I had a lot of clinical material relevant to missionary health and well-being and wondered what

Leaving Interhealth aged 70

to do with it. About this time I was introduced to Professor James (Jim) Watson, who expressed interest in the material and suggested we analyse it and get out a professional paper. He introduced me to the psychiatrist who has been my great friend and teacher ever since, Dr Dominic Beer. Poor Dominic – he had never met anyone who knew so little about writing professional papers, let alone statistics, but he was endlessly patient. It is important to insert here that in all research work of this kind I am careful to maintain the highest level of confidentiality. I abstract all the clinical material myself, individuals becoming merely part of the many statistics that such papers involve.

Dominic and I held our professional meetings in the student canteen at Guy's Hospital, and found it a great place to work. Once, however, we had to abandon ship! It was student Rag Week and the students poured into the canteen for a special variety programme. As time went by it appeared the next event would be a striptease, so we decided to evacuate. It took us some time to organise our material, but in the end we produced a paper on Expatriate Stress and got it published in a professional journal. I was indeed very grateful to God, Dominic and Professor Watson.

After the paper was published I realised there was still a lot of very useful unexamined information available. Dominic and I talked it over, and I went to see Professor Watson. We decided that it might be possible to gain further information and I could then work towards a London University MD. In the UK this is a higher qualification by thesis, rather like a sort of medical PhD, but not quite as grand. I chose the title *Expatriate Mental Health*, and began the long slog towards completion. In those days I frequently asked myself if this could be me! My brains were a bit addled by India, yet I was developing a vague understanding of statistics, learning computing to a reasonable level, wandering in and out of university circles, and learning how to use large professional libraries. What's more I was loving it. Slowly it all came together over the next few years. For the second part of the thesis I used a voluntary questionnaire to obtain information from people I had never met, and remain grateful to all who supplied me with such helpful material and gave me permission to use their comments anonymously. I was not surprised to find that the commonest cause of missionary stress was occupational problems. The second was children's education, this being mentioned specifically as the major child-related problem to be solved.

A few years later I presented my thesis to the two appointed examiners, and a few weeks later the day of my oral examination arrived. I had a minor drama just before the exam started. Being a polite lady I cleaned my teeth downstairs in the hospital cloakrooms, and quite forgot to put my dentures back in again. I looked okay as the dentures only supplied back teeth, but I would splutter as I talked, which would *not* be a good idea. I asked the young man I had been talking to if he would go down five flights of stairs to the cloakroom and see if he could find them. Just before the examiners called me in he dashed up waving an envelope. Someone had found the teeth and given them to the hall porter. So I popped them in, smiled sweetly and sailed in to face the ordeal ahead! They were satisfied with my thesis apart from one page of statistics which they asked me to repeat. My heart sank as I had absolutely no idea how to do it, but of course I said I would make the correction. I went home praying about it, rang someone up on the off chance she could find me a statistician and, within half an hour, the heads of two statistical departments in London teaching hospitals had said they would be delighted to help! So I went and saw the nearest one, the work took about 20 minutes, all was well and, after submitting the revision to the examiners, they informed me on my 78th birthday that I had passed.

My whole family, Monty, Vicky and Pat, my niece-in-law, sharing the day

Later on there was a marvellous university ceremony where those who had obtained higher qualifications had their academic hoods put on by a university big-wig. You had to kneel down on a sort of stand, and the hood was flung over your head to hang down your back, but I was so busy chatting to him that he had to say to me 'duck' so that he could throw it over! As I wrote in my prayer letter, 'Cinderella certainly went to the ball in a lovely scarlet gown with purple silk facings'. All in all, it was a wonderful day during which I breathed many prayers of thankfulness to God, Dominic, Jim Watson, my prayer partners and my ageing brain that had not let me down. Some time later I entertained all my family, Prof. and his wife, and Dominic and his wife, to a grand Chinese meal. Happy days indeed.

Writing a thesis of course necessitated my becoming computer literate, and again God provided help in the form of a computer expert called Ian Carter, later succeeded by Dan Morris. Both these were members of All Souls Church

Dr Dominic Beer, my faithful friend and teacher, sharing the day

and it was another occasion on which I found God's word to be true. He said that 'before they call I will answer', and both these helpful men turned up just when I needed them. I also joined a computer college in central London where tuition was done by giving the students disks to work through, and we could call for help if we got stuck. They had one student older than I was – a monk. He had been nice to work with, so when I turned up as an ex-missionary they were very welcoming, and both patient and efficient in their tuition.

Throughout this period I continued to travel widely. I have always relied on God's promises, and one that meant a lot in the next months was from the NIV version of Psalm 84: 'Blessed are those whose strength is in you, who set their hearts on pilgrimage'. My strength was certainly given to me by God so that I could complete the work he wanted me to do. I greatly enjoyed it, never losing the sense of astonishment that this was me, travelling, lecturing, writing, seeing people for consultations, all due to his loving care of me, the physical and mental health he had given me, and my willingness to obey what he asked me to do.

Looking back on my work, I realise what a privilege it was to do this rather unusual work. For example, in Peru I was able to see the work being done by national psychologists to help a group of very traumatised children who had fled with the surviving adults after the massacre of their parents. My driver for this period was

Working with refugee children in Peru

Lecturing to the Indian community in the Gulf countries

a converted get-away car driver – and although he was now a changed man, his driving was unchanged. I was petrified, but also rather enjoyed it!

Another interesting engagement was with a South Indian community working in the Gulf. They were opening a counselling

A day off to visit the Peak in Hong Kong

centre in their church and wanted some preliminary training work. I gave a whole series of lectures and felt so privileged to be there.

A little later on I went to Hong Kong. I met and interviewed many mission leaders and their staff, who were keen to know more about *Membercare* and some of the principles of selecting and caring for their missionaries. The organisation was superb and I enjoyed every minute of my stay, including a trip on the railway to the Peak from where we had a marvellous view of Hong Kong. By the end of this period I had visited over 40 countries, some of them more than once, and I remained so grateful to God for his endless help.

God's faithfulness to his promises emerged when I faced the problem of financing my travelling work. There was no way I could have financed it from the Interhealth salary and anyway this finished when I retired. Once more God did something wonderful. As a retirement present Ted and the Interhealth Board opened a Professional Trust for me to which people could contribute if they wished to support my work. As I indicated earlier, the Panahpur Trust kindly agreed to finance my travelling and research work for many years. I remain deeply grateful to them and, when my brother and sister died and left me enough money to finance my own work, I was glad to be able to release them from the arrangement so that someone else could be helped.

During these very busy periods of my life I remembered what I had learned in India and was very careful indeed to take adequate holidays. My sister and I went to Greece every year, to Cornwall every Easter and we had many other jaunts. I liked nothing better than going to her home on the train, having a lovely relaxed evening, then next morning climbing into her car and going off to Cornwall. I was the route-master and she was the best driver I have ever known, so we were able to explore some really tiny roads in Cornwall, often ending up on the moors. Such lovely experiences formed a pleasant memory bank that I could think about if things got a bit tough, or I was feeling somewhat fractious.

# 11

# The rapid growth of missionary care

After my retirement from Interhealth, and while I was completing my thesis, another new chapter opened for me, the development of Membercare, which I commented on in an earlier chapter. I mentioned that two American psychologists, Dr Kelly O'Donnell and Dr Dave Pollock were asked by the WEA (World Evangelical Alliance) to make missionary mental health and overall welfare a high priority. WEA was an international association interested in all aspects of mission, and various streams emanated from it such as the theological stream, and the missiological stream. We became the missionary care stream. We needed a title and, after a time, Kelly came up with Membercare. This was an important title, indicating that we were interested in more than just mental health. Although this remained our highest priority, our concern also included all forms of care such as quality of selection and training, and personnel support both overseas and on re-entry to the home country. Kelly became the full time worker in missionary care and Dave continued half time in his own private practice and half time specialising in the mental health of missionary children. He also had an increasing input into the needs of secular and Government expatriate mental health. They were a great pair and, as we worked together more closely, we developed a deep and caring friendship. Throughout the rest of my travelling career I sometimes bumped into Dave in an aircraft and the passengers were greatly amused by an aged lady swamped in the arms of a man with a large beard, hugging each other vigorously. He was a lovely man and we missed him so much when he died a few years ago.

Kelly began calling a small number of people together as an offshoot of the various conferences arranged by WEA. They were

We have missionary mental health conferences in lovely places.
Iguazu Falls, Brazil border

experiences I will never forget. Initially we were about twelve
people, including the local person hoping to set up Membercare.
The meeting in Nairobi, Kenya, was a classic example of the kind
of thing that was happening in other areas of the world. We sat
round a table for three days just talking about Membercare, what
it meant and what was needed locally. We spent a lot of time
talking, praying and just integrating. Dr Roger Brown, a local
missionary psychiatrist in Nairobi, was keen to start Membercare
formally in Kenya, so towards the end of our meeting we held a
special prayer session and then Kelly asked us to stand. We held
hands and asked God to bless Membercare Kenya – and so it was
born. The sense of God's presence was very real, and continued
to be so when we had the same sort of meetings in Malaysia,
India and Brazil. In Malaysia, Kelly, Dave and I held most of our
preparatory conversations in the swimming pool, a much-to-be-
recommended venue for future committee meetings. Kelly and I
had a good experience in India. We were staying in a newly built
hotel right on the outskirts of Bangalore, Southern India. One night
I wandered out in my very respectable housecoat to get a little air
on the terrace and found Kelly in his shorts running round and
round. So I joined him, and gradually the young people present
at the conference began to gather round to watch the strange sight
of two westerners, one decidedly aged and the other reasonably

United Nations Building, Kenya, lent to us for a missionary health conference

Before PowerPoint®, United Nations building, Kenya

young, shrieking with laughter as they ran round a roof terrace. What fun we all had together – I never saw the photos they took of us!

All these meetings and interviews with missionaries provided many of the facts I needed for both my thesis and for the second edition of *Honourably Wounded*. Of special interest to me has been the material relating to the 'new sending countries'. This is a global term and includes the many new countries that have begun to send missionaries either overseas or to different parts of their own countries. Their leaders are committed to providing good care for their personnel and the whole situation is very stimulating. It is important to remember that the newer sending countries do not have exactly the same problems as the older established missions, many of which were started in the 1800s. For example, in the newer countries major problems may arise from the monocultural nature of their own countries. In one organisation, this lack of experience of other cultures has been handled by giving mission candidates a short cross-cultural experience as part of their preliminary training, rather than leaving it to the post-arrival adjustment period. This had proved to be well worth while.

Handling family and social problems connected to national traditions may be a very difficult area for the new sending countries. In some cases, the person who wants to be a missionary is the same person on whom the family have built their hopes. Knowing that an adequate education could open the doors to a financially rewarding job, the family may sometimes have sacrificed a great deal to enable their child to be educated. The expectation is that he will then get a good job and so improve the family income. If their child wants to become a missionary, earning very little money, what are they to do? If they do not share their child's faith in God, a devastating hostility can develop between the parents and the prospective missionary, which usually extends beyond the family into the social community of which it is a part.

In a very small way I experienced something of the same financial problem. My mother was in full agreement that I should go to India as a medical missionary. However, I did not feel it right to go unless I could help her financially, and the very small missionary salary I would receive did not enable me to do this. Finally a friend who knew about my problem said she would provide the money for me to pay something regularly towards my mother's support, and she requested that I would never tell my mother about this arrangement. It all worked out very well and I could go to India with a clear conscience about my mother's welfare.

In some of the new sending countries another difficult cultural situation can arise when the person wanting to be a missionary is the oldest son. In these countries the eldest son is supposed to become responsible for everything concerning the family. One man I met explained things to me very clearly. 'Ever since I could understand anything,' he said, 'I knew I would have to be responsible for the whole family. I never seemed to be able to shake this off. It affected my studies and relaxation time, and now it is affecting my desire to be a missionary. I used to be so jealous of my younger brother who had so much free time, and could do what he liked.'

Language learning can be a problem for all whose mother tongue is not English, this being the *lingua franca* for most language schools. Various strategies have been utilised. Some sending countries give language tuition overseas through their own vernacular, combining this with a programme to strengthen their missionaries' English, but it is never easy to find a workable solution. Overall, as I talked with people from many different countries I became full of admiration for the care the leaders of the newer missions were taking as they set things up for their workers.

Bishop Jack and Mrs Hester Dain, my long term mentors and friends

Some time during this period I achieved the age of 80. My lovely All Souls Church fellowship groups organised a splendid party for me. I cannot start to describe how wonderful it was, and I am so glad my brother and sister were still alive to share in the fun. Guests included people from several parts of the UK and other European countries, Americans, Nigerians, Indians, Malaysians, and Chinese. Representatives from Interserve, Interhealth, All Souls and other places gave short talks, most of them recalling some funny incident. At the end I gave a speech, thanking God and all the people there for all they had done for me, and adding a few funny stories of my own. I was honoured that Bishop Jack Dain, my mentor from ZBMM days, was well enough to come and give the closing prayer and benediction – and then sadly we all had to leave each other and go home.

On the morning of my birthday I followed my usual custom of having a private communion. I have done this every decade since I reached my 50th birthday in India. I have always believed in rededication. It is easy to forget whom you are serving and to just plod along in the old routine. I find that an act of reminding myself of my commitment to God's service is a good thing, rather like a regular fresh start. Shortly after my birthday I read a verse in Jeremiah 30:21: 'Who is he who will devote himself to be close to me?' I stood up in my bedroom study and said out loud, 'I will and I do', and then I laughed because anyone watching me might think I was decidedly weird, although God understood what it was all about!

I remain so glad that the Bible provides me with words that lead me to think a lot of new things about God and that strengthen my faith. I fully believe that although there is a lot I do not understand, the core of what God wants me to know is in the Bible, and if with his help I can understand even a little of it, taking time to read it will be worth while. My pattern of reading it has not changed much. When I first became a Christian I used Bible reading notes to help me, but later on gave up the notes and began to study the text by myself, often in several translations. I developed the pattern of marking my Bible, writing comments, drawing arrows to link things up, and generally making sense of it that way. I use cheap paperback Bibles for this, buying a new one every year or two. Several books have been very helpful. For many years I have used the *IVP New Bible Commentary,* and a wonderful book called *Young's Analytical Concordance of the Bible.* This is a huge heavy brown book that explains the Hebrew and Greek meanings of all the words in the Bible. My other treasure is *Vine's Complete Expository Dictionary,* which explains the meaning of the Old and New Testament words used in the Bible. These have all travelled with me to India and Nepal and now live on my shelf in London, getting more and more battered as the years go by.

As an example of how God makes the Bible interesting, I recently decided to start 'a walk with Peter'. I read everything about him in the Gospels, the Acts and both his Epistles. My venue for part of this could not have been nicer, sitting reading behind a big coil of rope on the foredeck of a ship under sail and a little engine power at 6.30 in the morning in the middle of the Caribbean Sea! One of the things I realised about Peter was that his walk along the beach with the resurrected Jesus must have been a very important time. We do not know all that they said to each other, but I am sure they would have talked about Peter's betrayal. The Gospels tell us that after denying he knew Jesus Peter 'went out and wept bitterly', so obviously he would want to talk over the whole terrible event with the risen Jesus. As I studied further I discovered that however carefully I searched for it, Peter never mentioned his act of betrayal in his subsequent writings. It dawned on me that I was looking at an amazing result of God's forgiveness. It was so powerful, and Peter's acceptance of it was so complete, that he never needed to mention it again. Jesus had paid the price for sin on the Cross and Peter could now accept that he was forgiven, and that the episode was in the past. Because of his own experience Peter would be specially enabled to lead the young Church into a greater understanding of the pathway to forgiveness and newness of life, and I doubt if he ever forgot he was now a man whose past sin of betrayal had been 'wiped out' by God. He indicates this in Acts 3:19 when he spoke to the crowds just after he had healed a crippled beggar. 'Repent then and turn to God, so that your sins may be wiped out', he said. Vine explains that this means 'smeared out completely' or 'washed out'. I found the thought very meaningful. So often we keep raking up our past and all the things we did wrong, when God wants us to confess it all, be forgiven, put right what we can, then leave it with him. Where irreparable harm has been done we can never undo this, but I believe by our deep repentance and his forgiveness, healing can come to even the worst of bad situations.

Apart from exciting Bible studies, what next did God want to do in my life? I was 80 years old, and as I write this I am now 85. I am in good health, suffering from a little forgetfulness of names but otherwise mentally not too bad. I am still able to walk long distances, travel, lecture and look after everything in my home. The major thing is a new sense of freedom. I have realised that while getting old has its handicaps, it also frees you to do all sort of odd things. For example, last year when I was praying about my future service God put into my mind the thought that I should be 'nice' on the London Underground. Hardly anyone is nice on the Underground, especially at rush hour. It has proved to be a most interesting experience. I do not know if I am really doing a work for God or just enjoying myself, but travelling around London and other parts of the world has become quite exciting. I have been polite, asking people who look lost if I can help them, and if I have time I take them to the area they are looking for. When we part I often say 'God bless you' and they smile! However, I do try to remain sensitive to the need of tired travellers to sit and read the paper without talking to anyone, because there is nothing worse than turning into an interfering busybody!

Sometimes very interesting conversations open up, and I have met some lovely people. One of the most recent was a Nigerian teacher who was visiting the UK again after having worked here some years ago. She turned out to be a committed Christian, and as she left the carriage we hugged and kissed each other, much to the surprise of the other passengers. I also met a West Indian woman who travelled from East to West London every Sunday to pray with a small group of people. The interesting thing is that when we part so many say to me, 'Thank you for speaking to me'.

Another group I have met is 'the Hugh Grant group'. Hugh Grant acted in the famous film *Notting Hill*, and in one scene climbed over a garden gate to canoodle with his girl friend on a wooden seat, 'canoodle' being a local word for 'hugging and kissing'. This gate leads into a private garden to which I have a key, so if I see people standing looking longingly over the gate I offer to take them in. After a good look round the garden they sit on what I hope is the Hugh Grant seat to have their photos taken. I met a lovely honeymoon couple from Birmingham who were thrilled to have a good canoodle on the seat as I took their photo. One Chinese group was discussing something in a rather agitated way at the end of our garden visit and I realised they were talking about how much money to give me. I explained none was needed – I was glad to help them. I thought they would never stop bowing! In this rather *ad hoc* ministry I am fully aware of the need to be cautious, but because I am so obviously old and harmless I have never had any trouble.

Although I have found all this very interesting and it may, perhaps, help to reduce a fraught atmosphere in a crowded place, I have often asked myself if this is a 'ministry', or if I am just having fun. Some time ago I remembered that God has made our bodies the temples of his Holy Spirit, as Paul explains in 1 Corinthians 6:19. I began to understand that God allows us to take him with us as we move around the world. I also remembered that one of the gifts of the Spirit is 'helps'. We are therefore sometimes enabled in our ordinary daily lives to show people that God loves and cares about them. We cannot always 'say so', but we can 'show so', to coin a phrase. So until God tells me to stop I intend to continue my small ministry of helping and maybe some to whom I give travel advice may want to talk a little about the God I serve.

I still have a little professional involvement. I am on the board of a new free journal we send to various parts of the world to keep people in touch with developments in mental health

Debbie Lovell-Hawker, my successor in missionary health care

care. We have received some very interesting papers that others will find really helpful. I continue to meet the people whom God has called to further the development of Membercare. In the UK he has provided Dr Debbie Lovell-Hawker, a psychologist who is planning to spend the larger part of her time looking after missionaries. She has travelled widely, is an excellent seminar leader and lecturer, and a skilled listener and counsellor. Another of God's provisions is Marion Knell who is an expert in expatriate children's problems as well as carrying administrative responsibility within the developing Membercare structure. Missionary mental health care and selection interviews continue in the able hands of Dr Sharpe and the psychologists at Interhealth.

So I am now redundant in my old roles – and am happy to be so. I still give a few lectures and lead seminars, and continue to have a role in Membercare and other conferences worldwide, but attend these as 'everybody's grandmother'! This is a very happy position to hold, and I find it helps to be old, and to be independent of any formal mission membership. It makes me safe to talk to.

Last year I had a brief period of joining three different countries in their annual Christian medical student conferences. It began with my giving a special lecture at the annual UK conference, and at the end I was asked by the students to attend their own conferences in Norway and Latvia. The Norwegian one had very beautiful and profitable evening sessions. The whole hall was lit by candles, music was played and a well prepared programme flowed without announcement. I shall never forget the last evening. All of us who spoke at the meetings were asked to take part in a foot-washing ceremony. The students who wished to share in this came into a tent near the entrance and we spoke to those who sat in front of us – and then washed their feet. I tried

En route to Norway student conference

to give everyone a special verse to take away. In the conference room five altars had been created, and we could wander round and do various things at each one. They were all lovely, but one especially remains in my mind. It was a wooden cross with a heap of stones nearby. You were invited to tell Jesus about any problem you had, or to confess something to him. You then picked up a stone and put it at the foot of the Cross to indicate you accepted he had forgiven you and that, now you had 'cast your burden on the Lord', he would sustain and guide you. The service flowed on without announcement, a mixture of music, dance, Bible reading, a few words of encouragement and help, and prayers. After the benediction no one moved. So the band went on playing and people went in and out of the counselling tent where the foot-washers were waiting to help them. Most of the people just sat quietly in the meeting room and it was an absolutely wonderful experience of love, peace and fellowship.

After a short interval at home, I went to the first Christian medical students' conference in Latvia, attended by students from three countries. I had little role other than mixing with any students who spoke English, but right at the end I gave a talk on depression. It was a great privilege to be there. These are the first generation of students since the Russian occupation ended and I had a strong sense of this being an historic occasion. When they discovered that I could use a computer, had a digital camera and owned a mobile phone, they immediately christened me Techno-Granny! I have had several other titles, like 'Doctor Miss Sahib', or 'that woman who lives up the back staircase near the church', but I think I am the most proud of the Latvian one.

In the academic area, Dominic Beer and I are now planning a new research programme on 'Homesickness in Missionaries'. Many groups have been studied since the topic first emerged in the literature in 1678, but not missionaries, so it will be interesting to see if anything helpful comes up.

I do not know what God wants next, but am happy to work it out with him day by day. I have many thoughts about the last move from earth to heaven and feel increasingly certain that it will be an entry into a new sort of freedom and service. I do not know for sure, of course, but I feel that our involvement with earth will not cease until the earth itself finishes, although this involvement will be on a different pattern. We do not know much about what life in heaven will be like, other than the knowledge that we shall be living in the presence of God and experiencing all the beauty and power of the Trinity. We shall 'know and be known' as the Bible says. But I doubt if I will ever lose my surprise that God picked me up. I wonder if in heaven I will still continue to be amazed that this is really me, here and alive in the actual presence of God. God really did love me enough to turn me to himself all those years ago and to come into my life. He has continued to enable me, to forgive me when I mess things up, and to use me in all sorts of surprising ways. In those early rather desolate years I could never have imagined anything remotely like this and I will indeed be saying a very big thank-you to him for all he has done, and for all the friends he provided as part of his loving plan to help me during the various stages of my time on earth. They have been fabulous and I could not have done without them.

A fairly recent development concerns my family. One of the penalties of being a single missionary and living away from home for many years is that things move on for both you and the family you left behind. Going home on leave helps, but all sorts of events occur in which you have had no part. Relatives marry, babies are born and, if you are away long enough, they themselves marry and in the end you hardly know any of them. I was fortunate in that my brother and sister-in-law, and my sister and her son, all came to see me from time to time, but even so there was a lot of catching up to be done on final return. God has really honoured his promise to 'set the solitary in families'.

The Fraser family – my nephew Malcolm and his wife Sandra, and their
daughters Amanda and Jennifer

My brother and sister died within ten months of each other
in 2002 and 2003, and it was all rather bleak for a time. However,
as we prepared for the funerals, I had a real bonding opportunity
with my sister's family who live in USA and my sister-in-law's
niece Pat. We are all the best of friends. They visit me and I visit
them and once a year at least my nephew Malcolm and I go away
for a week together.

Pat and I see quite a bit of each other and one of my best
experiences is when I go to her home in the summer, sit on the
patio in her lovely garden and *relax*. I can feel the tension oozing
out of me. Malcolm is a doctor, as is his lovely wife Sandra, and
they have a son and two daughters. The son does computing work
and one daughter is a medical student. Both are doing very well
indeed. The other daughter is just finishing her first university
degree where she also has done very well in both her academic
studies and athletics (running). She has fulfilled all my own
frustrated ambitions. I was a student in the war years when we
had little opportunity for sport and, other than Nepal where we
walked everywhere, in most of the countries where I worked women had few sporting facilities. So the best I can do now is to try
to walk the London marathon course, starting the day after the
race and taking three to four days to cover the 26 miles. I go home
at night of course to sleep. But my great-niece does the real stuff,
running in relay races for her university, and I try hard not to be
too envious. However, two years ago I ran the ancient course at
Olympia and have a photo to prove it!

# Conclusion

The title of this book, *Can it be Me?*, expresses my surprise at finding myself doing all sorts of things I would never have thought possible and, as I conclude, I think this needs further comment. Since I read a review of *Honourably Wounded* on the Internet I have been a little apprehensive about writing this final section. Basically the writer was favourably impressed with the book, but ended, 'When I read her comments on the scriptures I reminded myself not to make amateur psychological comments when I speak about the Bible'. However, another reviewer did say I had 'sane Biblical insights' so I have plucked up my courage.

The amazement I have expressed in this book is not the same as the irritating phrase Christians sometimes use when talking about their lives – 'It's not me, it's all of God'. Christians are certainly not just God's automatons. In reality, God begins to live and work with us in partnership as soon as we accept the forgiveness that Jesus accomplished for us on the cross, and ask him into our lives. Our freedom of choice is never overridden by a dictatorial God, although mercifully he sometimes puts things on 'hold' until we have seen a better way to accomplish his loving purpose for us.

For example, when I was asked to leave Nepal and go back to India I could have said 'No'. My excellent mission would ultimately have accepted my refusal, but after a time of anger, grief, and prayer, I felt sure that I should agree to return to India, however hard it was for me to leave Nepal. It proved to be the pathway to new growth, and it amazes me that this is one of the things that happen when we follow his choice for us. For the rest of our lives he never stops working with us, strengthening what is weak, smoothing out our rough edges, helping us during the bad times and sharing our enjoyment during the good times. Best of all, he will always pick us up with loving forgiveness when things go wrong and we turn to him in despair. He has an infinite number of new beginnings within his loving kingdom.

As I write this I am humbly aware that I am speaking of the Lord of creation, the God of all power, who chose to live in partnership with us because he made us and he loves us. Psalm 139 outlines this very clearly: 'You created my inmost being, you knit me together in my mother's womb, ... your eyes saw my unformed body, all the days ordained for me are written in your book before one of them came to be'. This does not mean we have no choice, for he is prepared to wait patiently until we are ready to do his will. This is made very clear in John 3:16, which explains that God loved the world so much that he gave Jesus to die for our sins and so bring us back to himself. It then goes on to explain that 'whoever believes in him will not perish but have everlasting life'. The word 'whoever' indicates that we have a choice and can accept or reject the amazing possibility of living in partnership with God. As Revelation 3:20 says, God 'stands at the door of our lives and knocks'. He never forces an entry, although he may give us several clear reminders to do something about it. I know that my life would not have been the same if I had never understood that I was responsible for deciding what to do about God's offer. The last part of the passage explains this: 'If anyone hears my voice and opens the door I will come in and eat with him and he with me'. Our opening of the door of our lives is where the partnership starts, and these days I often imagine the glorious picnic we shall have when we go to him in the heavenly places.

In this book I have repeatedly indicated how important the Bible has become to me and I am thankful for the day I decided that I would accept it as God's word to me, try to understand it, and to live by it. One of the first phrases I began to think about after I became a Christian was 'the promises of God'. I had to discover what this meant. As I read the Bible I found that God made many promises to his people, which he intends to keep. For example, the author of Hebrews reminds us of an ancient promise from God, and asks us to apply it to ourselves. In Hebrews 13:5, in the context of learning to be content with what we have, the author writes, 'God has said, "Never will I leave you, never will I forsake you"'. That takes a time to think about, but if we believe it we can move on to accept verse 6, 'The Lord is my helper, I will not be afraid. What can man do to me?' Human beings may do a lot of bad things to each other, but in God's hands a loving outcome is sure, although not always in this world. I needed to cling to this when I visited Rwanda about a year after the troubles and saw the piles of massacred bodies still half-filling three large churches. I asked myself why so many of God's servants were killed. I do not know, but I still believe the promise that 'he will never leave us nor forsake us', and that ultimately God will ensure that something hugely valuable will emerge from such horror.

I have already described the first time I 'stood on a promise' after the ward service in Exeter when God enabled me to speak. I took the plunge, and trusted then, as I still do, that his grace was indeed sufficient for me because his strength was being made perfect in my weakness. Doctors and other helpers have never enabled me to speak without stammering or to read aloud freely, but in my many speaking engagements God has put his hand on me, and has helped me speak well enough to get over what he wants me to say. In London I have constant encounters with Indian people, we usually switch to the vernacular when they find I can speak it, they compliment me on my accent and we have great times together. Who would have thought it!

This was all summed up for me in a hymn I discovered very early on in my Christian life, and still sing occasionally in my prayer time.

> Standing on the promises of Christ my King,
> Through eternal ages let his praises ring,
> Glory in the highest I will shout and sing,
> Standing on the promises of God.
>
> *Chorus:*
> Standing, standing,
> Standing on the promises of God my Saviour,
> Standing, standing,
> I'm standing on the promises of God.
>
> Standing on the promises that cannot fail,
> When the howling storms of doubt and fear assail,
> By the living word of God I shall prevail,
> Standing on the promises of God.
>
> *(Chorus again, and so it goes on.)*
>
> R. Kelso Carter (1849–1926)

I have thought a lot about the meaning of my basic turning to God in 1942. In the café in Exeter, Norah Nixon taught me why

God had met me that evening in church, using the verse I have already discussed, John 3:16. However, I do not think I came to God from a sense of sin, although I sometimes felt guilty for being alive, but I had this huge need to belong, to be loved in a new way. My parents did love me, but it all got clouded by their troubles. God's love never changes or gets clouded by events. He really, truly, loves us. When I stood up in the church that night I was indicating to God that I wanted to enter his kingdom, and I believed he had received me and had come into my life. I had been what the Bible calls 'born again'. Norah's use of John 3:16 confirmed that the next day. I brought to God massive needs, and at the same time dedicated to him some of the gifts he had given me. I realised he had given me persistence, conscientiousness, a deep enduring love of history, literature, music and the natural world, and the ability to study and to write down clearly what was necessary for my professional work. In return he gave me the faith and courage to believe that what God had written was true, that it applied to me and should be acted upon.

When God began to teach me a lot of new things during my illness in Lucknow, I learned the importance of keeping 'short accounts' with God. I remembered something that is actually rather amusing, but which illustrates an important principle. When I write it down it sounds a bit like what we used to call 'nit-picking', paying attention to trivia, but in reality it was part of a pilot plan for the life ahead of me. It is a very simple little tale of stealing and lies for personal gain, without a qualm of conscience. When I was a little girl I was in the Brownies, the junior Girl Guide movement. Every week we had to take one penny to the meeting to pay for the equipment we used. This was a small coin but it meant a lot to our impoverished family. As I went to Brownies I passed the sweet shop, and there in the window were chocolate drops, which I *loved*. You could get quite a reasonable number of them for one penny, so I told my mother I needed two pennies for Brownies because the fees had gone up, which was a lie. When she kindly began to produce two pennies for me to take, I spent one penny on chocolate drops and gave the other one to the Brownies as per usual. I did this for nearly two years, and the weekly chocolate drops, which I ate before going home, were absolutely delicious!

The fact that God reminded me of something I had totally forgotten seemed to me significant and I realised this account had become a long one! Whether or not it was nit-picking I didn't care – I wanted my dishonesty to be forgiven and recompense made.

So, I added up the approximate amount I had falsely obtained, added ten percent interest, and sent the money to my mother, who was both startled and amused at this late repentance for a childhood dishonesty.

It has a much deeper relevance than being just a little story. For example, after a quarrel we often allow anger to fester within us to the point where it is doing us harm. Sometimes a move from our side may be all that is needed to put it right, so that a relationship can be restored through honesty, repentance and forgiveness. Even if it doesn't work, we have at least tried. I fail God many times, but one of the important things I have learned is to say sorry as quickly as I can. Then his promise can come true that, 'If we confess our sins he is faithful and just to forgive us our sins and to cleanse us from all unrighteousness'.

Another important aspect of Christian living that needs to be mentioned is the problem of finding time to study the Bible and to pray in our very busy lives. It is easier now that I can plan my own days, but I learned several important things during my working years that are applicable to us all. Although we value the prayer patterns of our churches, we also need to 'deformalise' praying. Sometimes as young Christians we think we need to 'pray properly' – and initially some guidance can be very helpful. Basically, however, the important thing is that we talk to God. This needs no formality, although many of us do like written or formal prayers as a part of our worship, but we can also learn to talk to him as freely as Brother Lawrence did. He burst a bombshell in the Christian world when he described practising the presence of God in his kitchen and talking to him as he worked. There are times in our spiritual lives when we are overcome with awe and just have to remain silent. But side by side is the knowledge of the constant presence of God wherever we are, and our freedom to talk to him briefly between patients, or while we rush from one office to another, or in the few minutes when the kids have mercifully gone for a short sleep. This is what I meant when I wrote earlier of learning to 'pray on the hoof'. I learnt this as a young doctor when I was on prolonged call due to shortage of staff and I was so grateful for understanding it when I became hyper-busy in Lucknow and Nepal, or when I have been rushing around in airports for too long. He is with us and in us in a realistic way, as Jesus promised when he spoke to the disciples of the coming of the Holy Spirit – 'He is with you and will be in you'. So in our working day we can have periods of remembering his greatness and majesty, while at the same time enjoying his companionship. 'I am with you always' and 'I will never leave you nor forsake you' really mean something in this context.

In our desire to learn more we need short cuts to profitable Bible reading. I tried to set aside a day every three months when I was in Lucknow so that I could really get down to more prolonged Bible study and prayer, but for the day to day needs I relied on 'Daily Light', later published in modern translation as 'Living Light'. This book gives collections of verses on a particular topic for every morning and evening of the year. I could read this quickly, and then carry a verse around with me to chew over in short intervals between patients. Sadly they are both out of print, but pressure is being applied by many of us for a re-issue.

I love singing hymns so whenever I had a few minutes alone or was walking to a new area of the hospital I would sing a verse or two (very quietly!) and feel much better. So there are ways and means of keeping fed spiritually, but we may have to lose some of our preconceived ideas about what is the 'correct' thing to do. I value correctness, but there are times when we should give it a rest and branch out.

So there we have it, a troubled child whom God met, who usually, but not always, co-operated with the growth patterns God had in mind, who failed many times but was picked up and happily re-employed in God's kingdom. It may be an unusual thing to say, but I feel so satisfied in God. Note that I am not writing 'satisfied *with* God' – that would be the deepest presumption I could think of – but I am deeply satisfied by the opportunity he has given us to live a human life in partnership with him. I love my family and friends, the work I do, and my hobbies and interests, but the basis of all this is a deep certainty of God's loving purpose for me ever since I first gave myself to him. This was his basic purpose for all of us when he took the trouble to come to earth as a baby, teach and heal, go to the Cross to bear our load of guilt and sin, and rise again to prove himself a living triumphant force in face of much evil.

Can it be me? Thank you, it was and it is.